Take

A

Walk

Through

The Bible

Embark on a colorful journey through the Bible

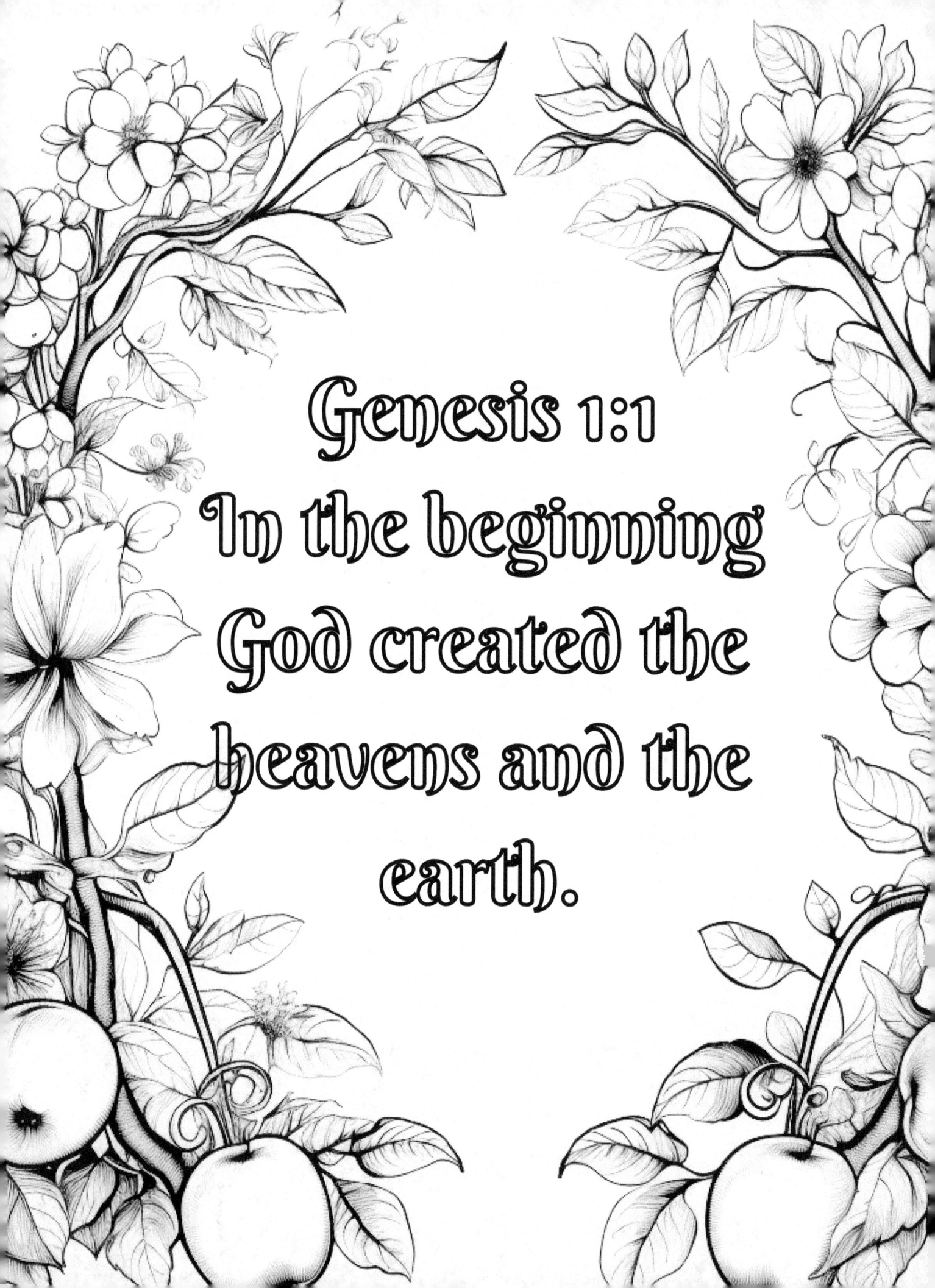

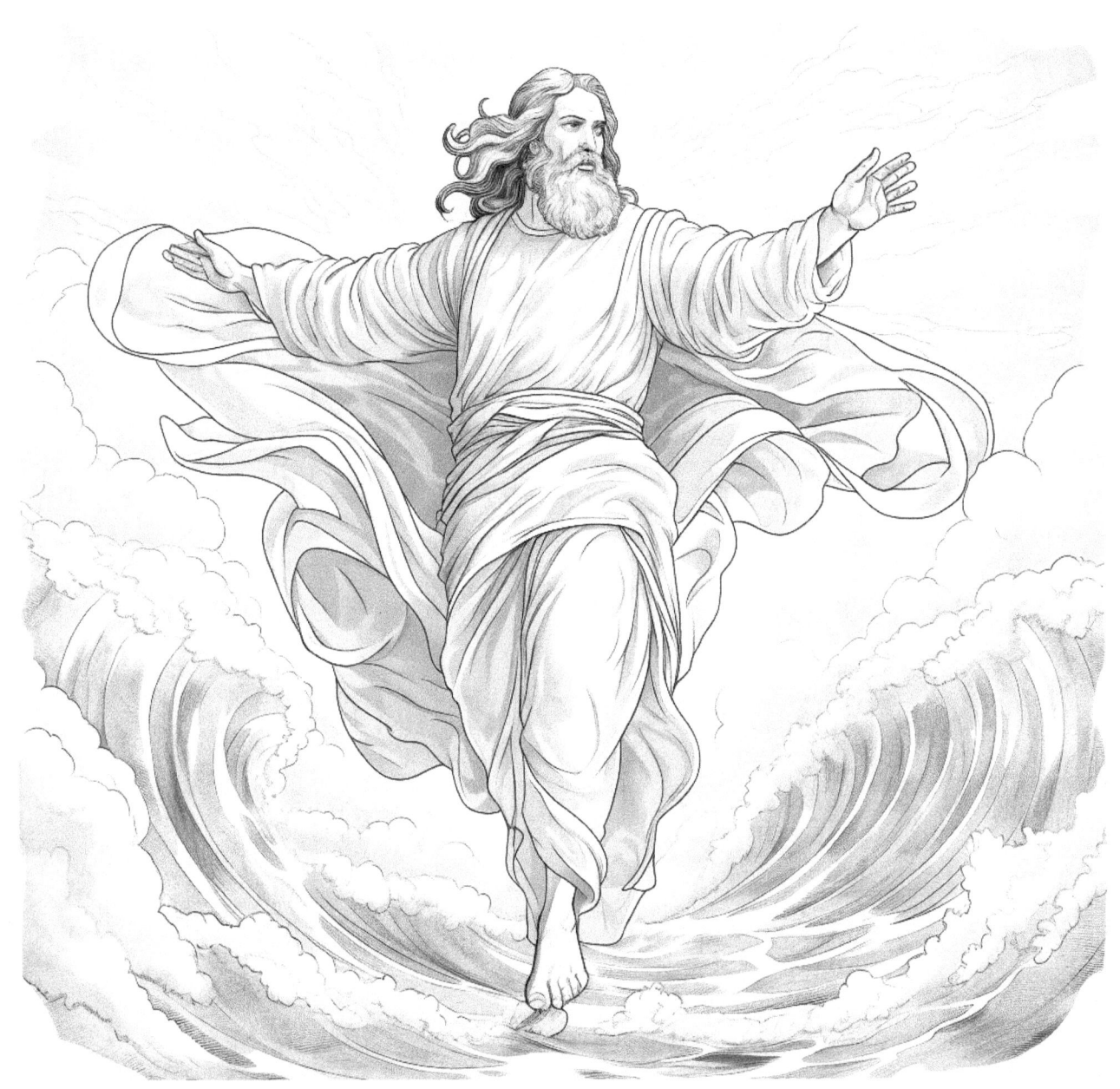

2 Now the earth was formless and empty, darkness was over the surface of the deep, and the Spirit of God was hovering over the waters.

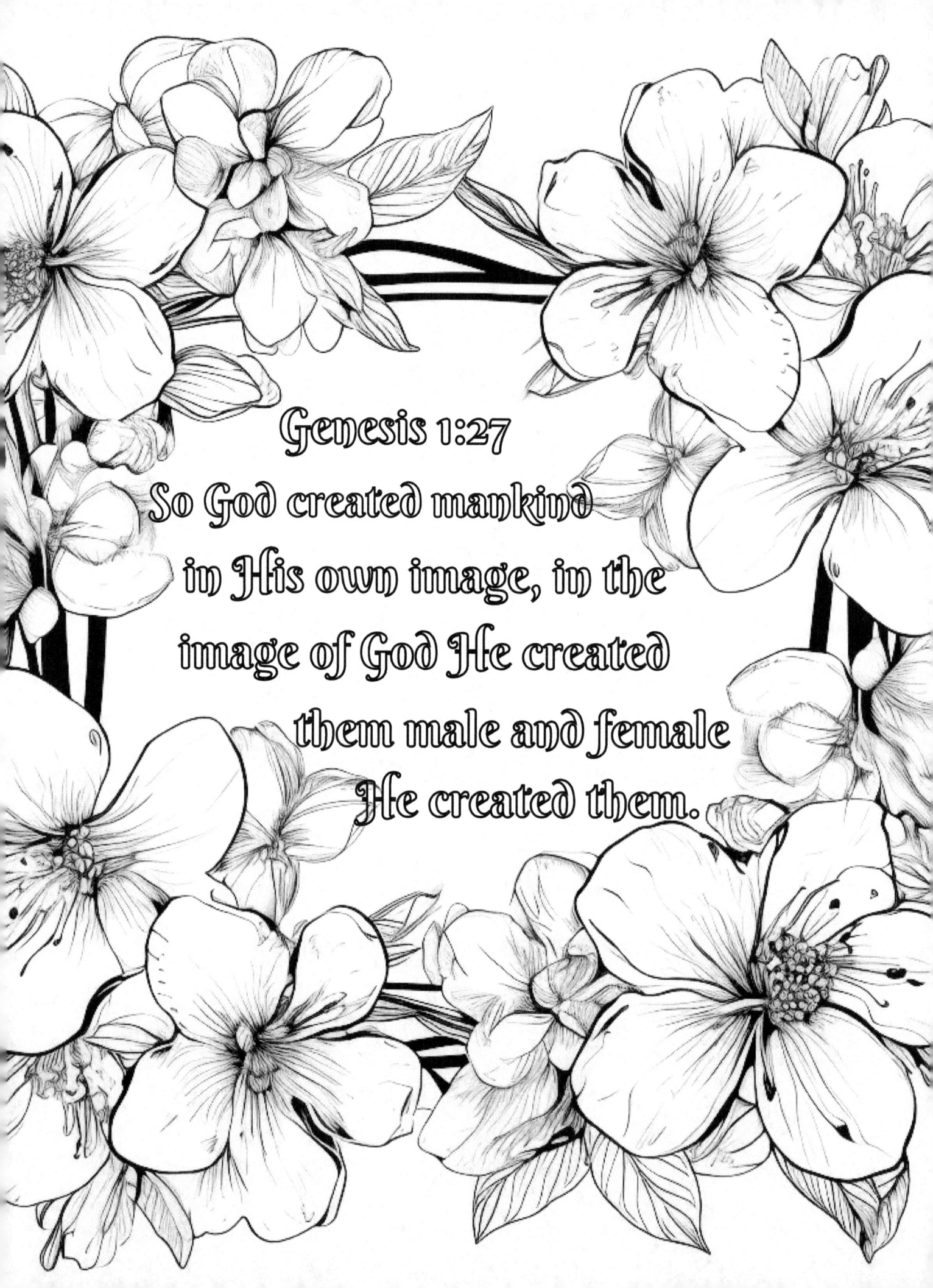

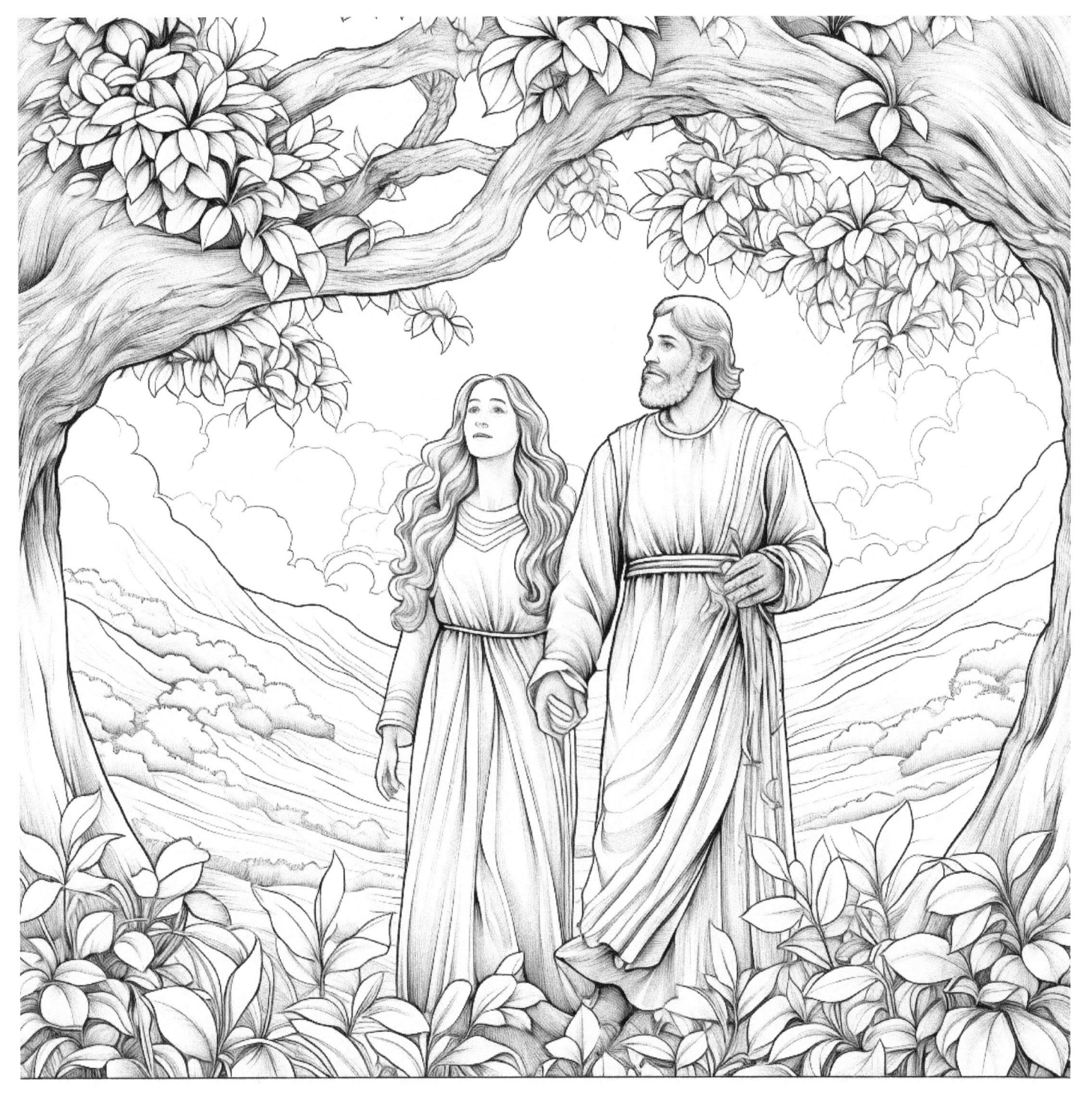

Gensis 1:31 God saw all that he had made, and it was very good. And there was evening, and there was morning—the sixth day.

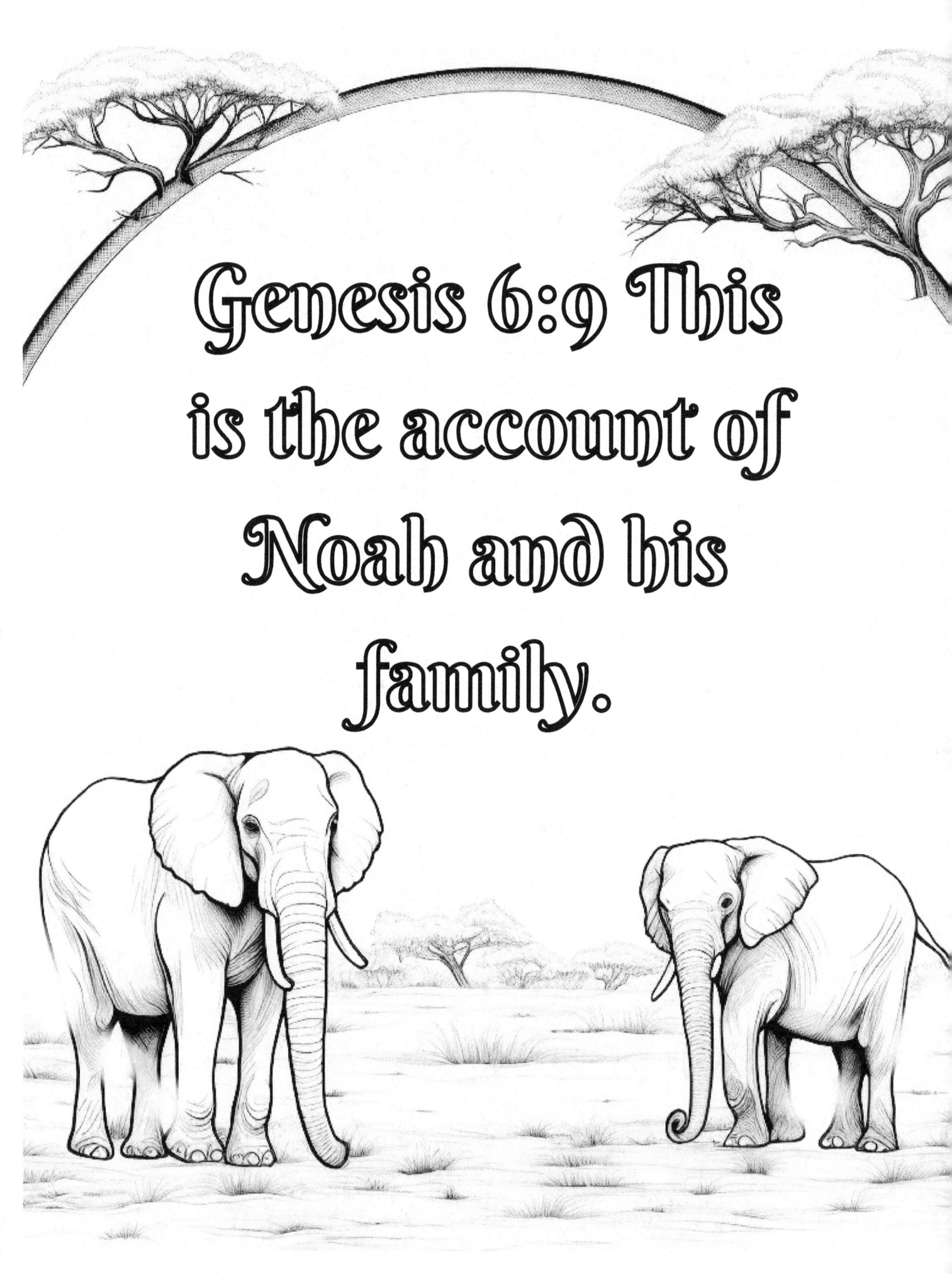

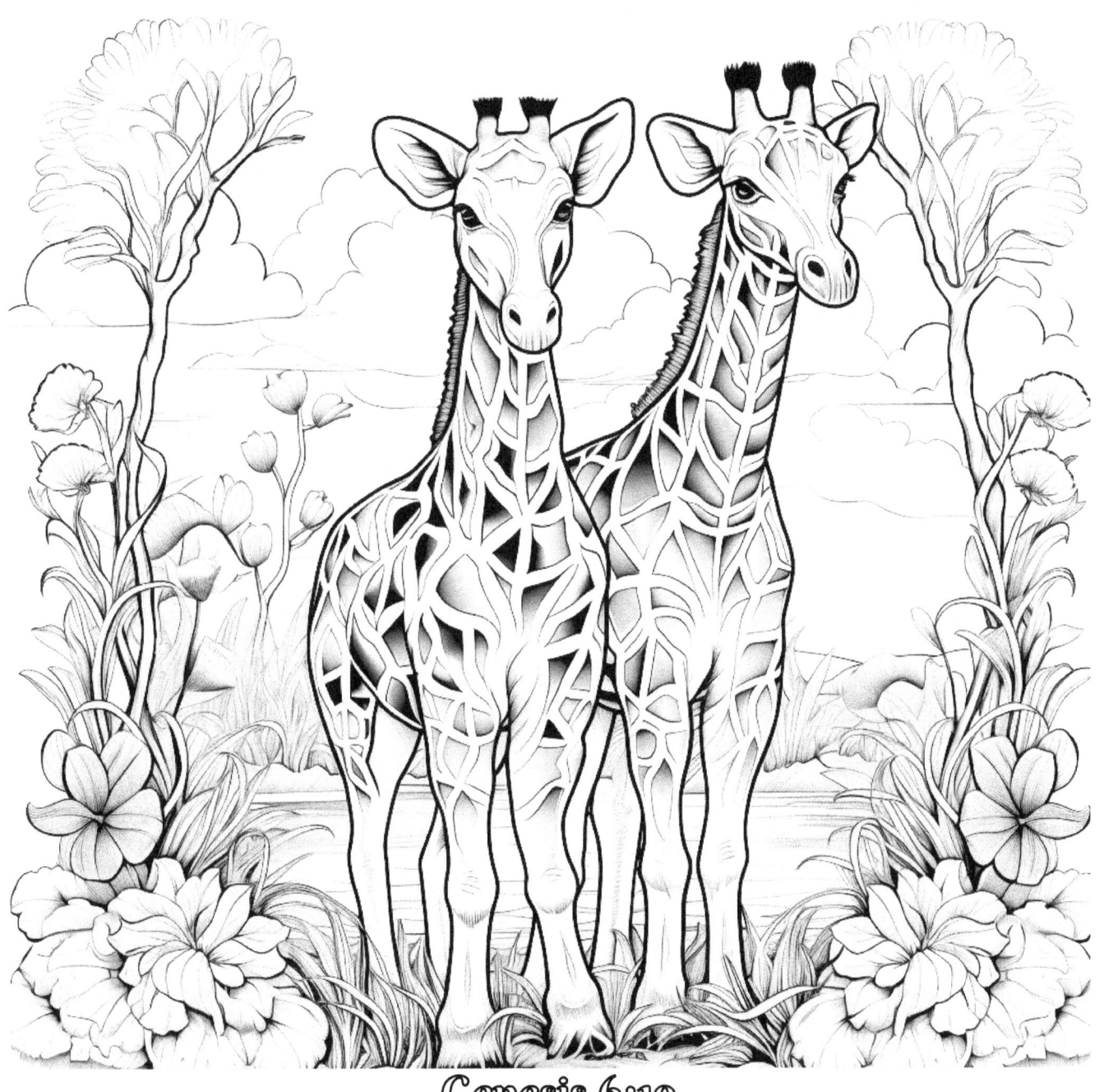

Genesis 6:19

"You are to bring into the ark two of all living creatures, male and female, to keep them alive with you. 20 Two of every kind of bird, of every kind of animal and of every kind of creature that moves along the ground will come to you to be kept alive. 21 You are to take every kind of food that is to be eaten and store it away as food for you and for them."

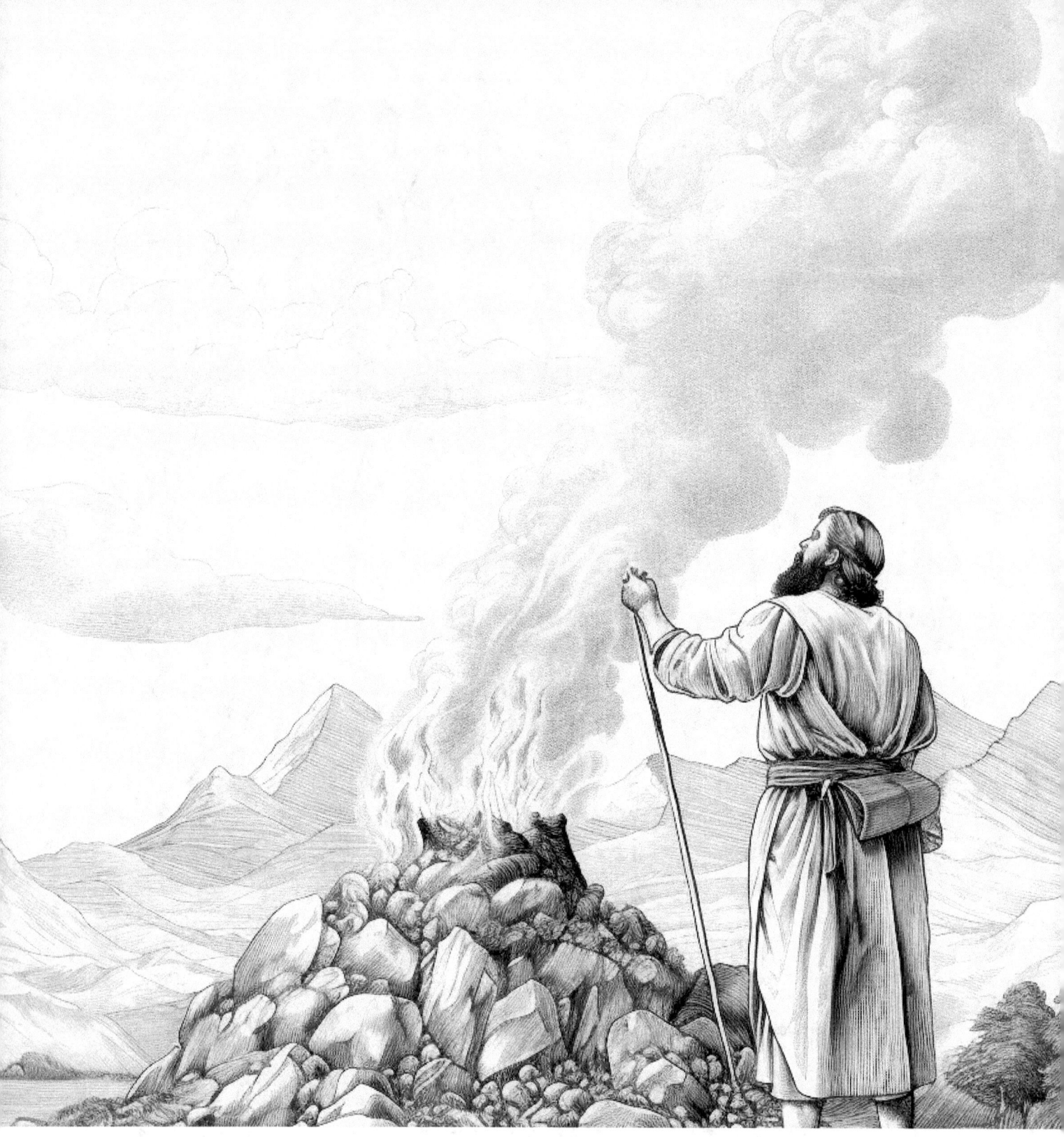

Genesis 22:2   Then God said, "Take your son, your only son, whom you love—Isaac—and go to the region of Moriah. Sacrifice him there as a burnt offering on a mountain I will show you.

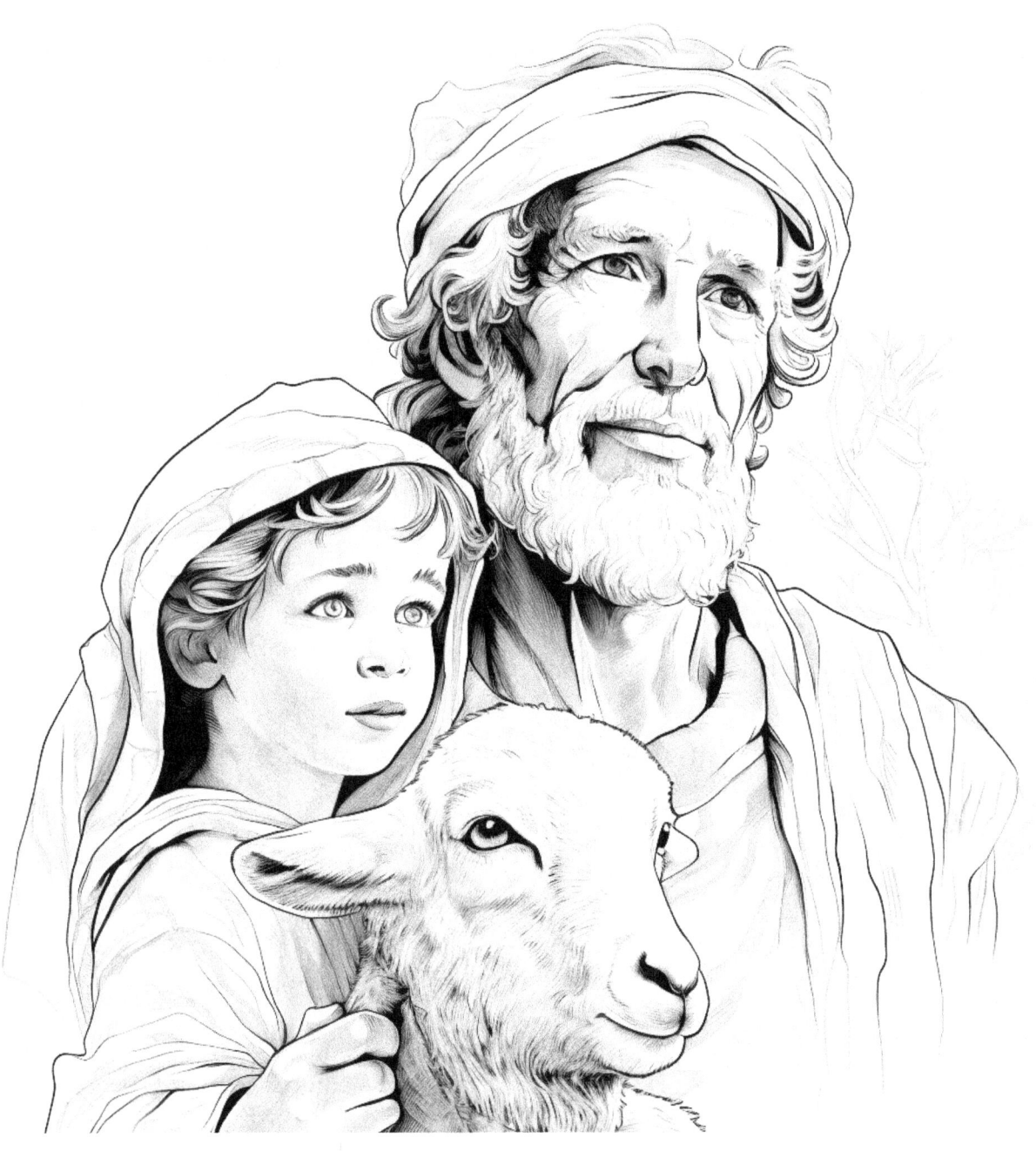

Genesis 22:17

I will surely bless you and make your descendants as numerous as the stars in the sky and as the sand on the seashore. Your descendants will take possession of the cities of their enemies,18 and through your offspring all nations on earth will be blessed, because you have obeyed me."

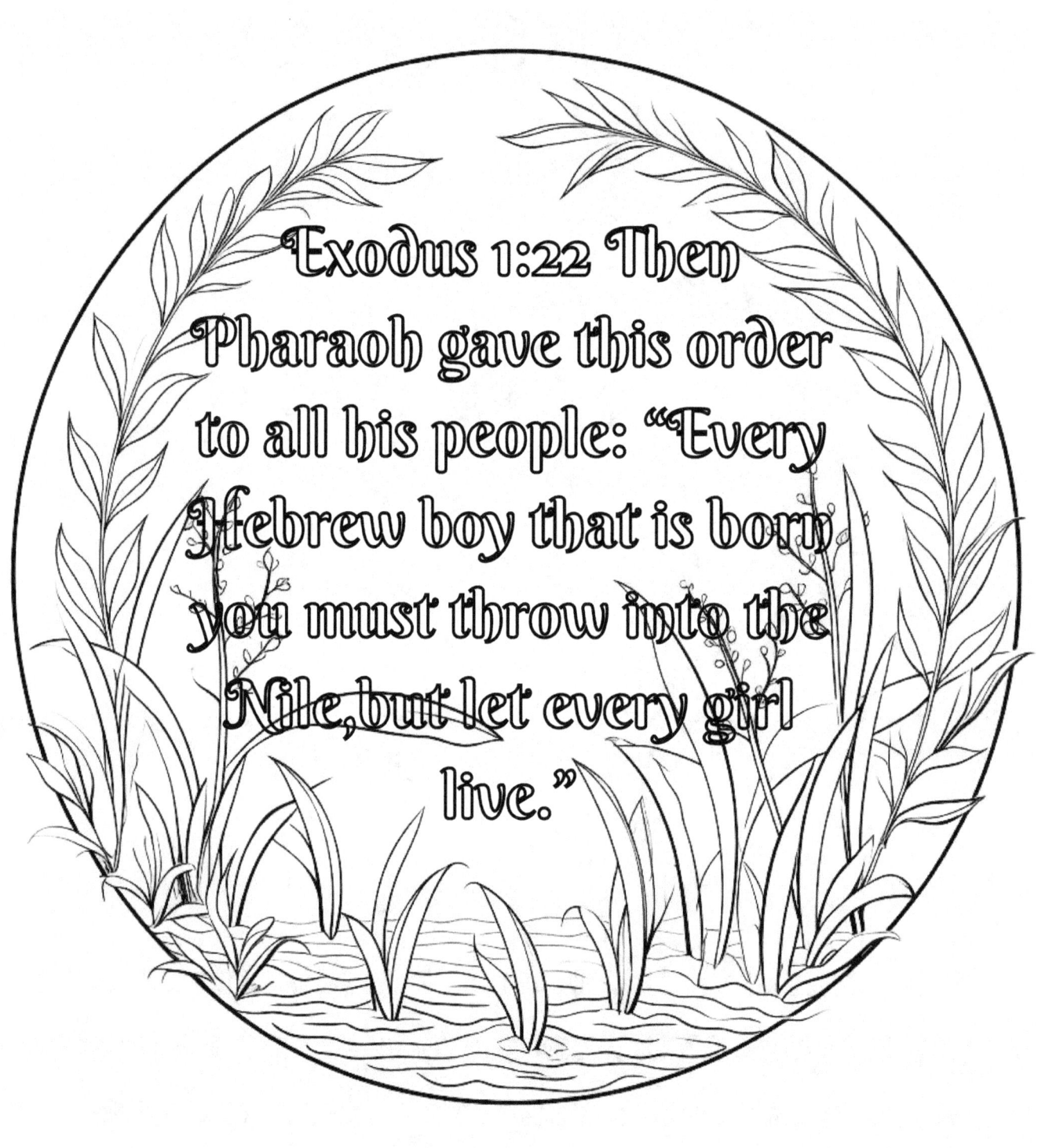

Exodus 1:22 Then Pharaoh gave this order to all his people: "Every Hebrew boy that is born you must throw into the Nile, but let every girl live."

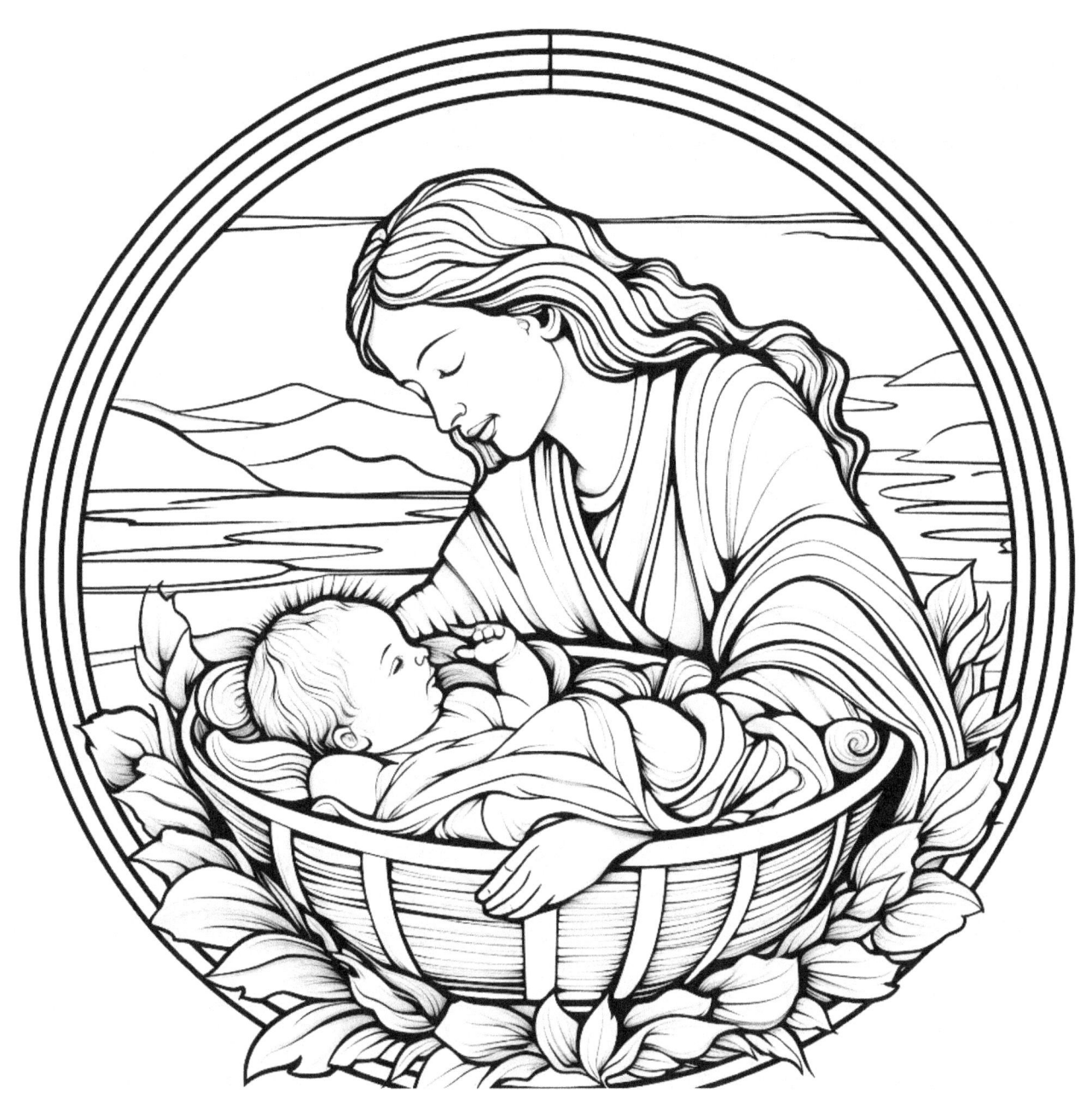

Exodus 2:6 She opened it and saw the baby. He was crying, and she felt sorry for him. "This is one of the Hebrew babies," she said.

Exodus 20:2 "I am the Lord your God, who brought you out of Egypt, out of the land of slavery.

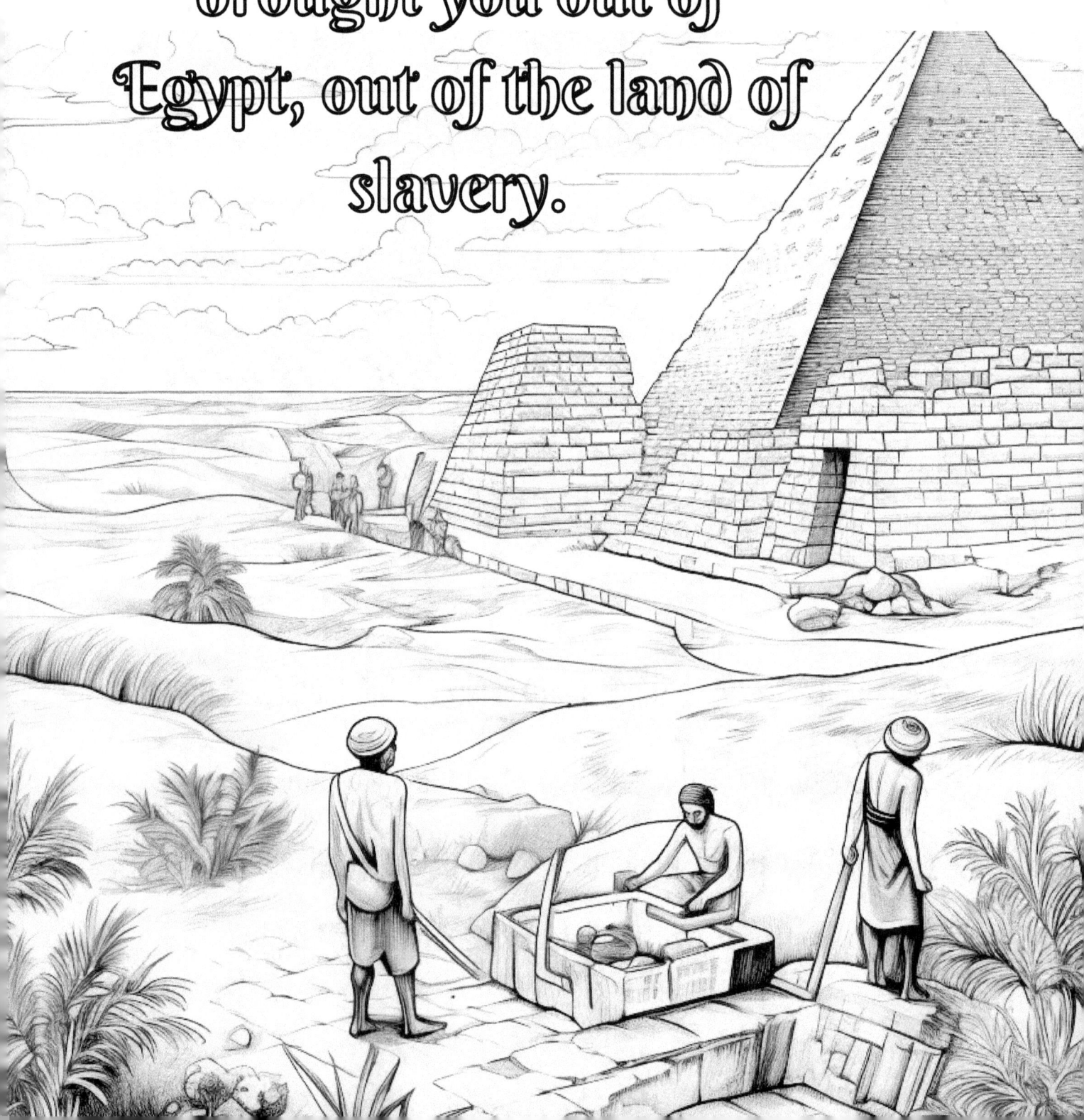

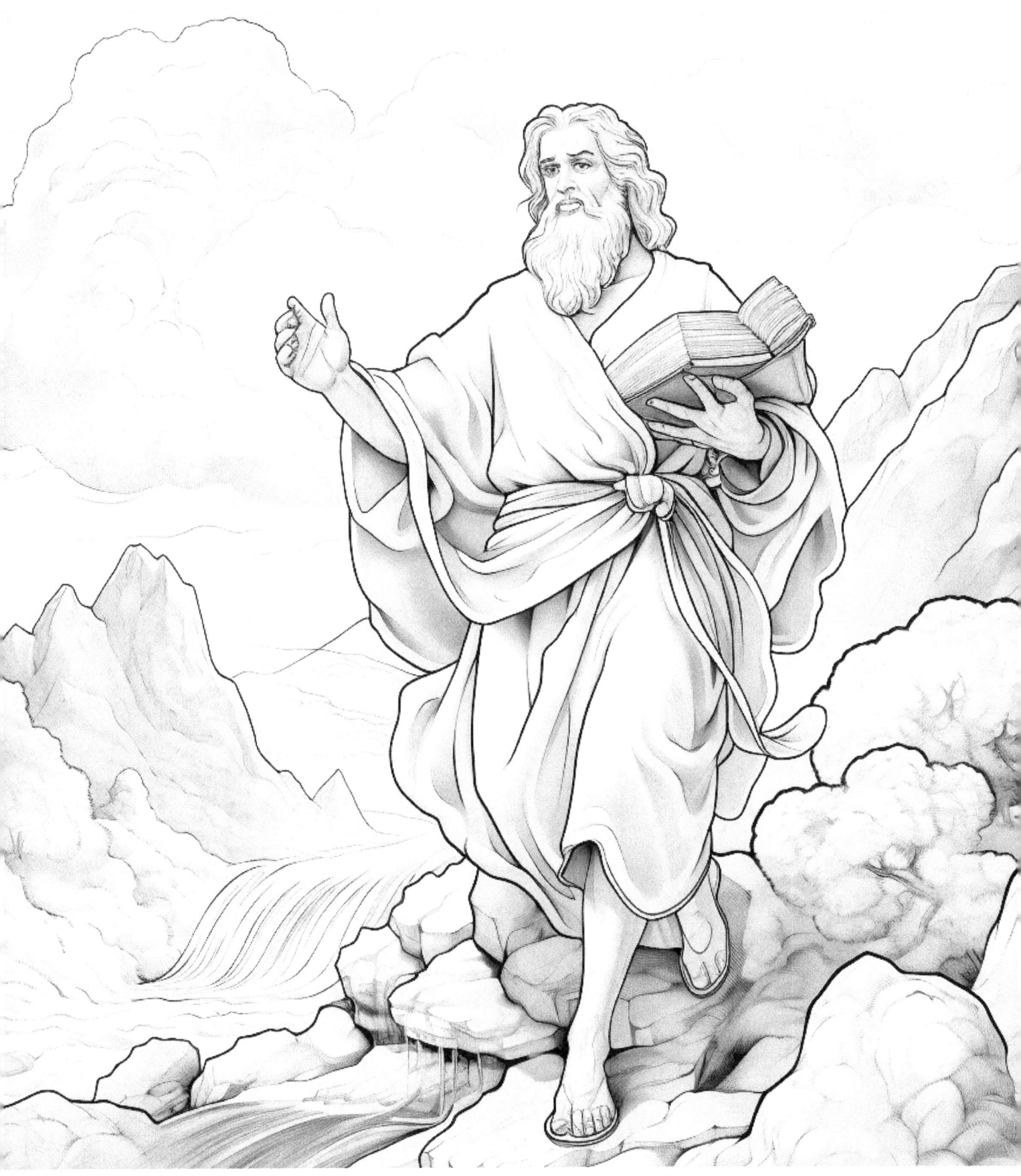

Exodus 20:3 "You shall have no other gods before me.

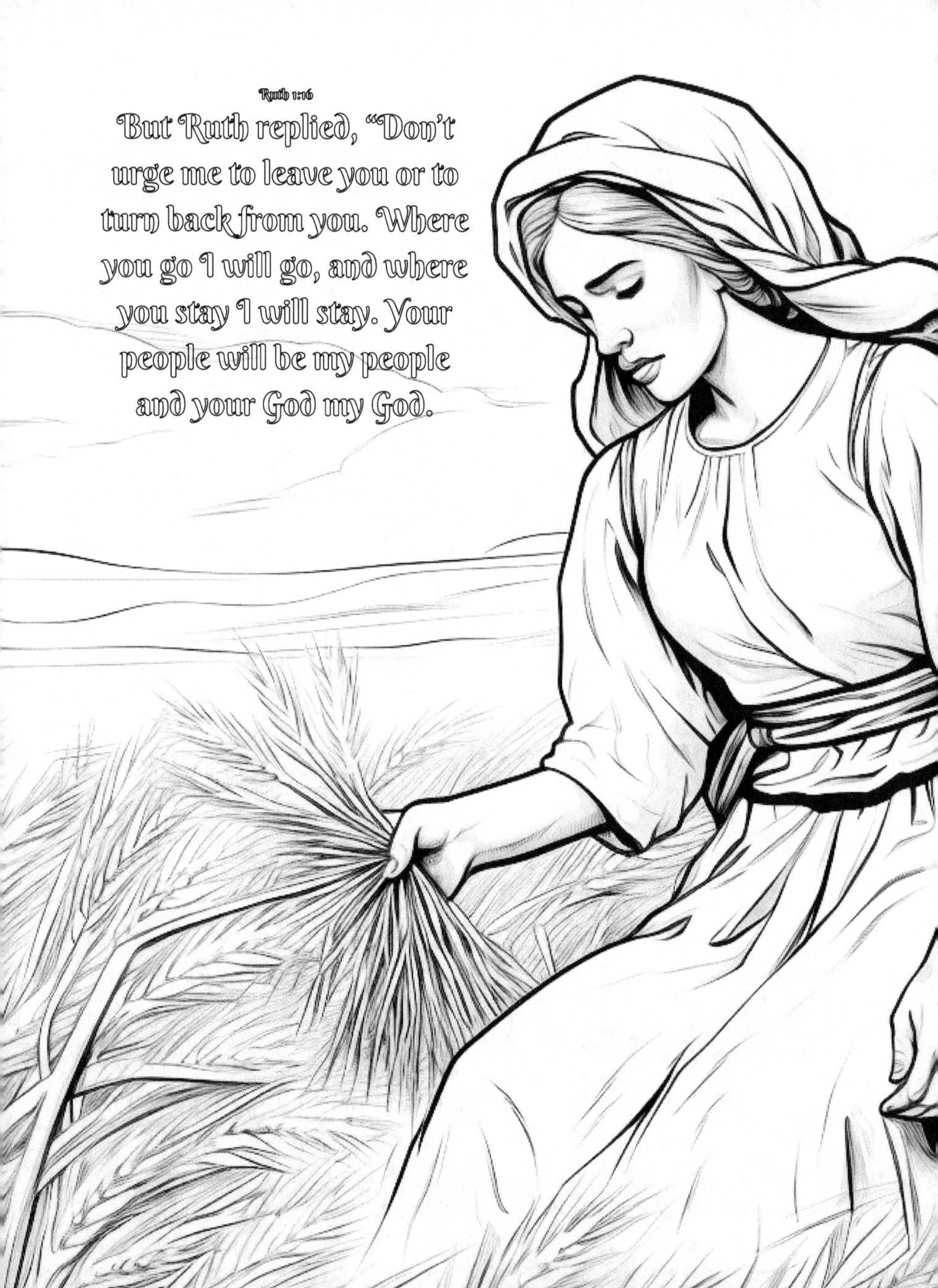

Ruth 1:16

But Ruth replied, "Don't urge me to leave you or to turn back from you. Where you go I will go, and where you stay I will stay. Your people will be my people and your God my God.

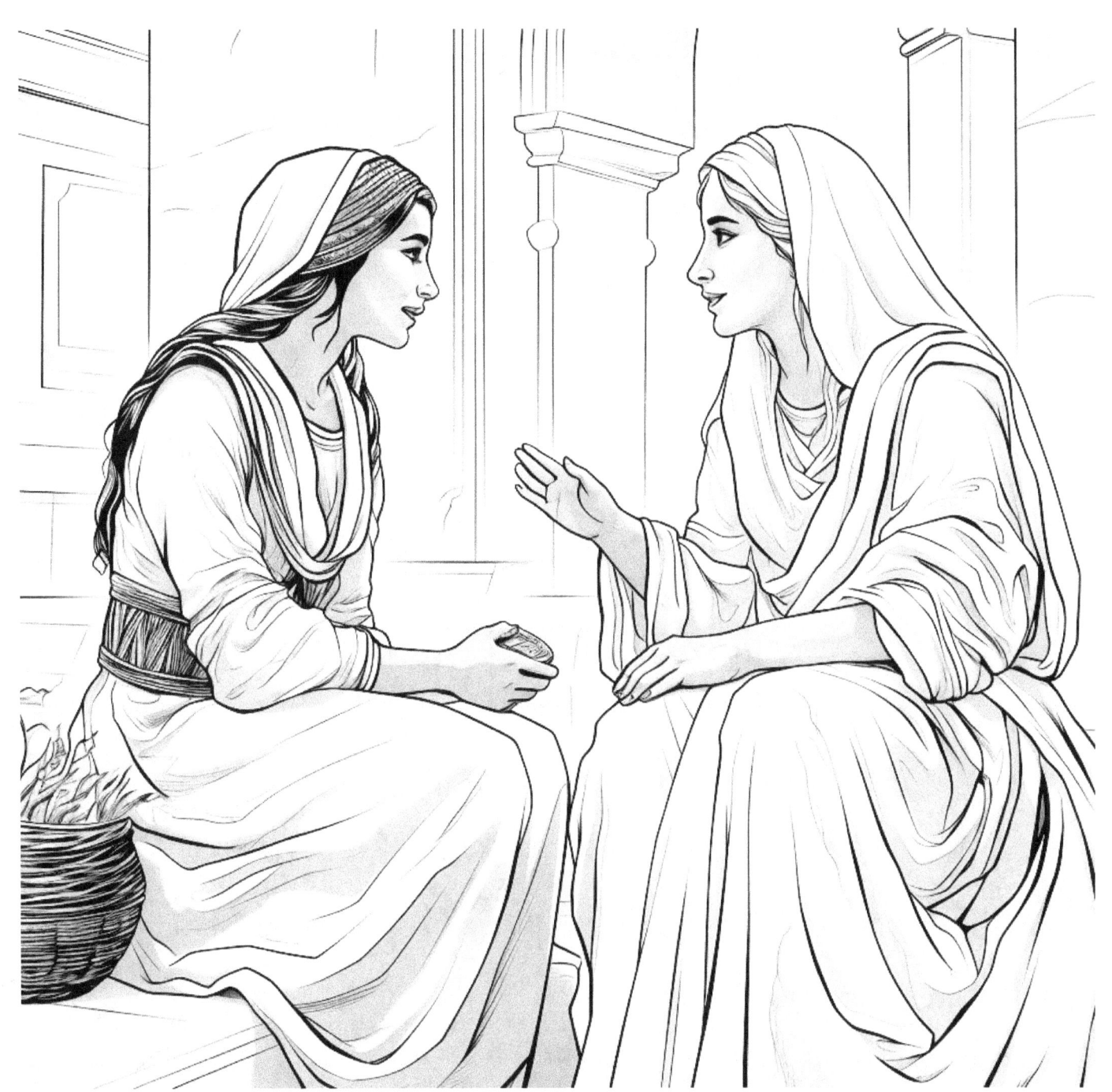

Ruth 1:17 Where you die I will die, and there I will be buried. May the Lord deal with me, be it ever so severely, if even death separates you and me."

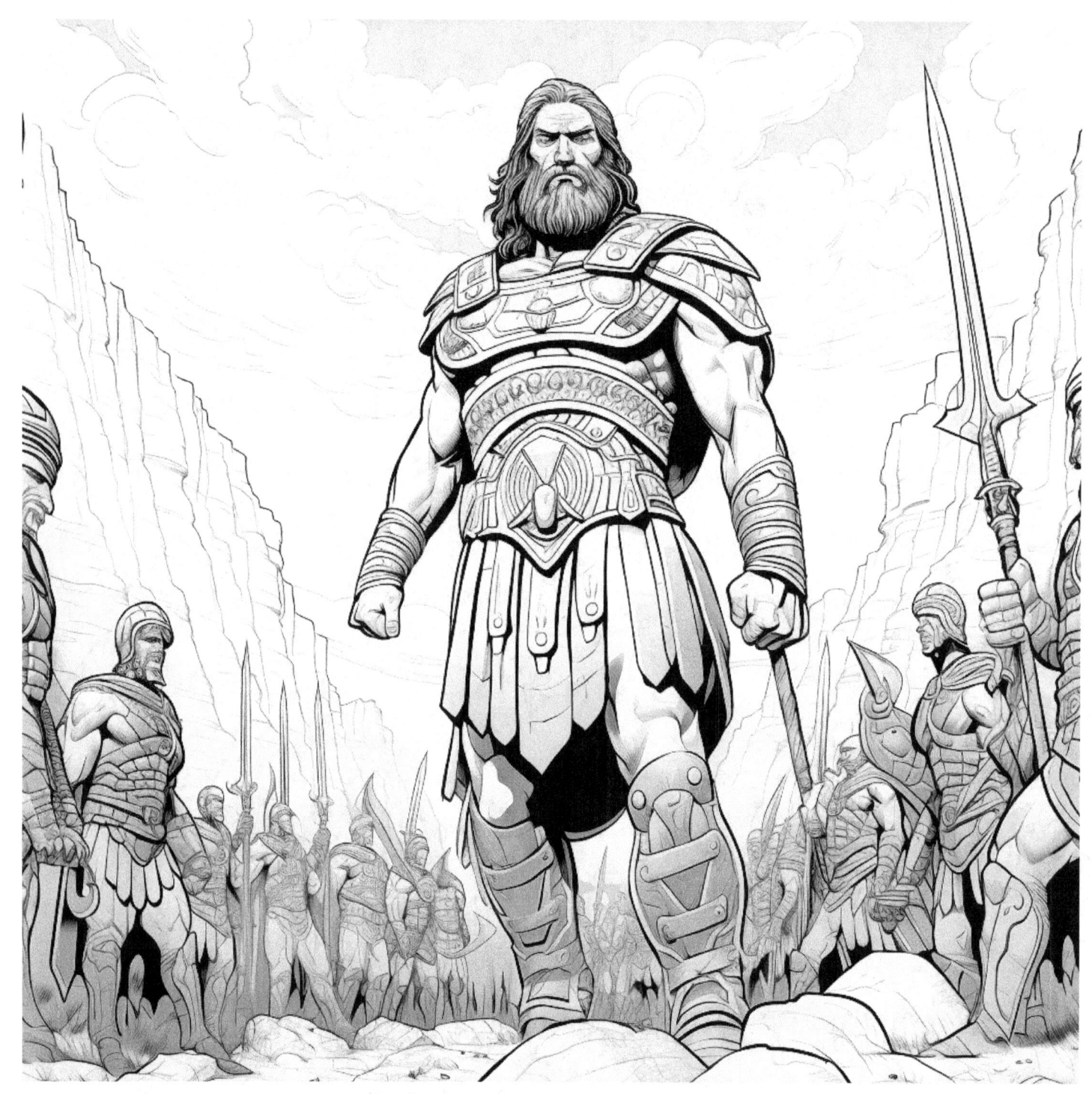

1 Samuel 17:45 David said to the Philistine, "You come against me with sword and spear and javelin, but I come against you in the name of the Lord Almighty, the God of the armies of Israel, whom you have defied.

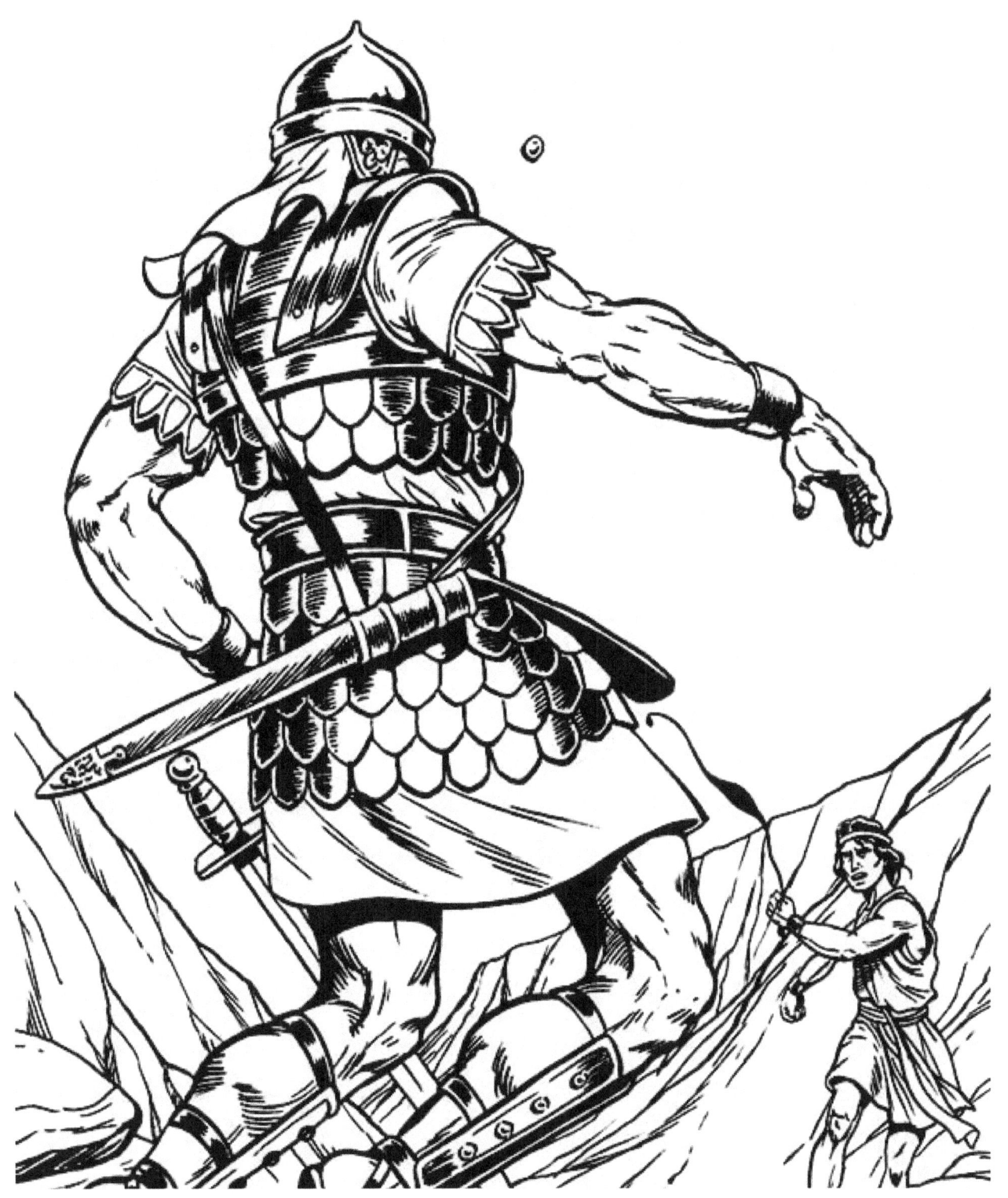

1 Samuel 17:47 All those gathered here will know that it is not by sword or spear that the Lord saves; for the battle is the Lord's, and he will give all of you into our hands."

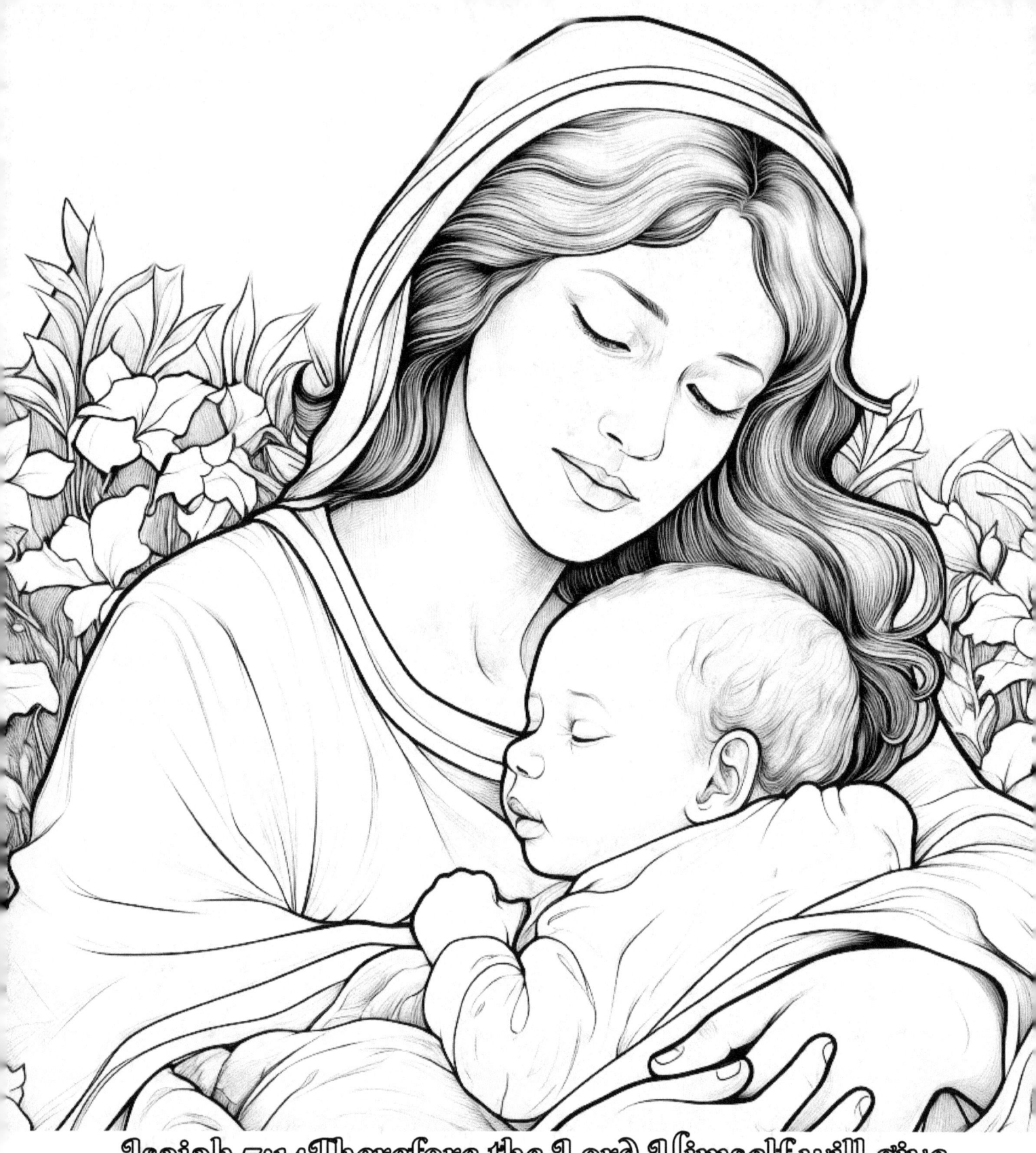

Isaiah 7:14 Therefore the Lord Himself will give you a sign: Behold, the virgin shall conceive and bear a Son, and shall call His name Immanuel

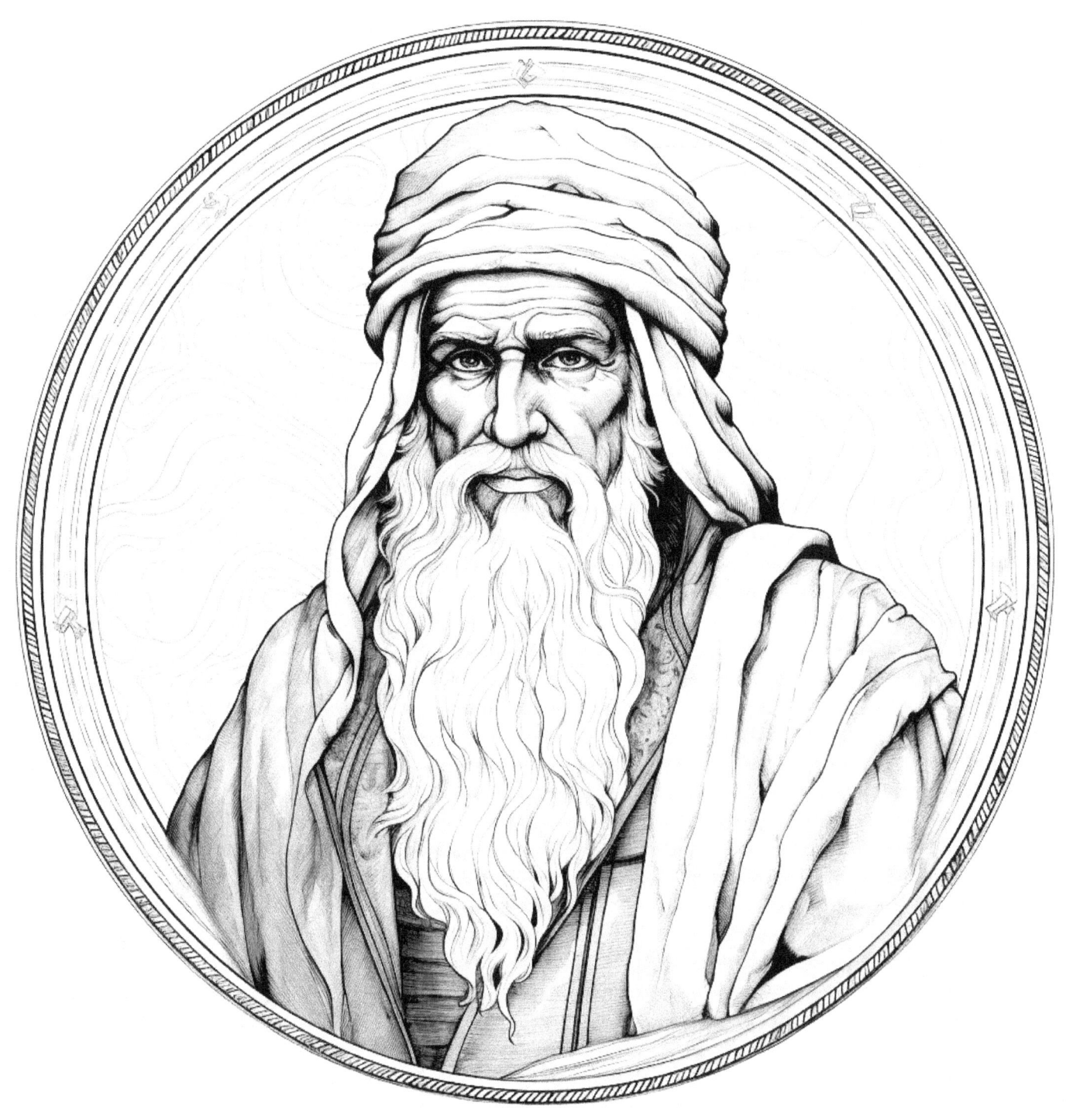

Isaiah 7:15
Curds and honey He shall eat,
that He may know to refuse the evil
and choose the good.

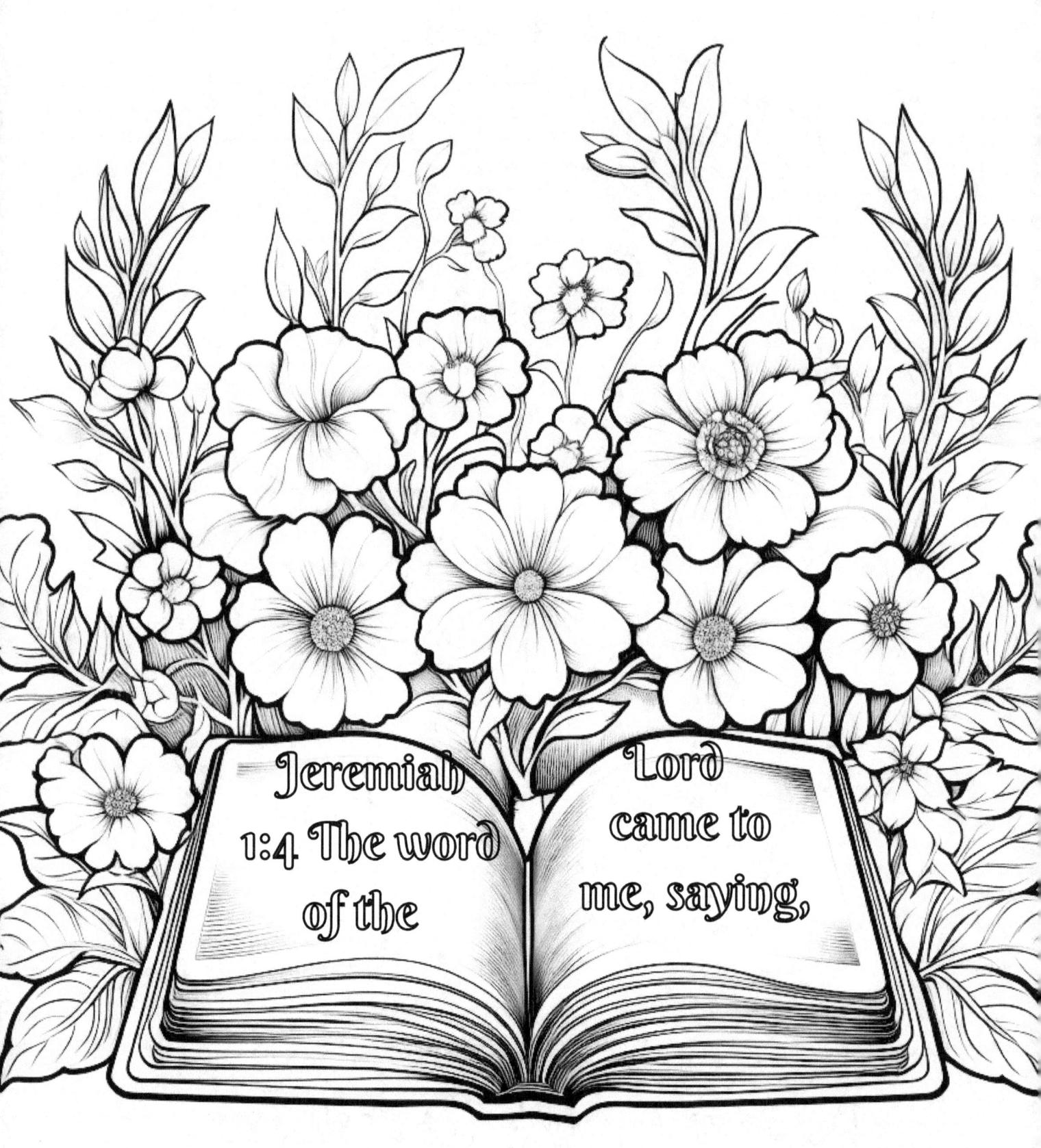

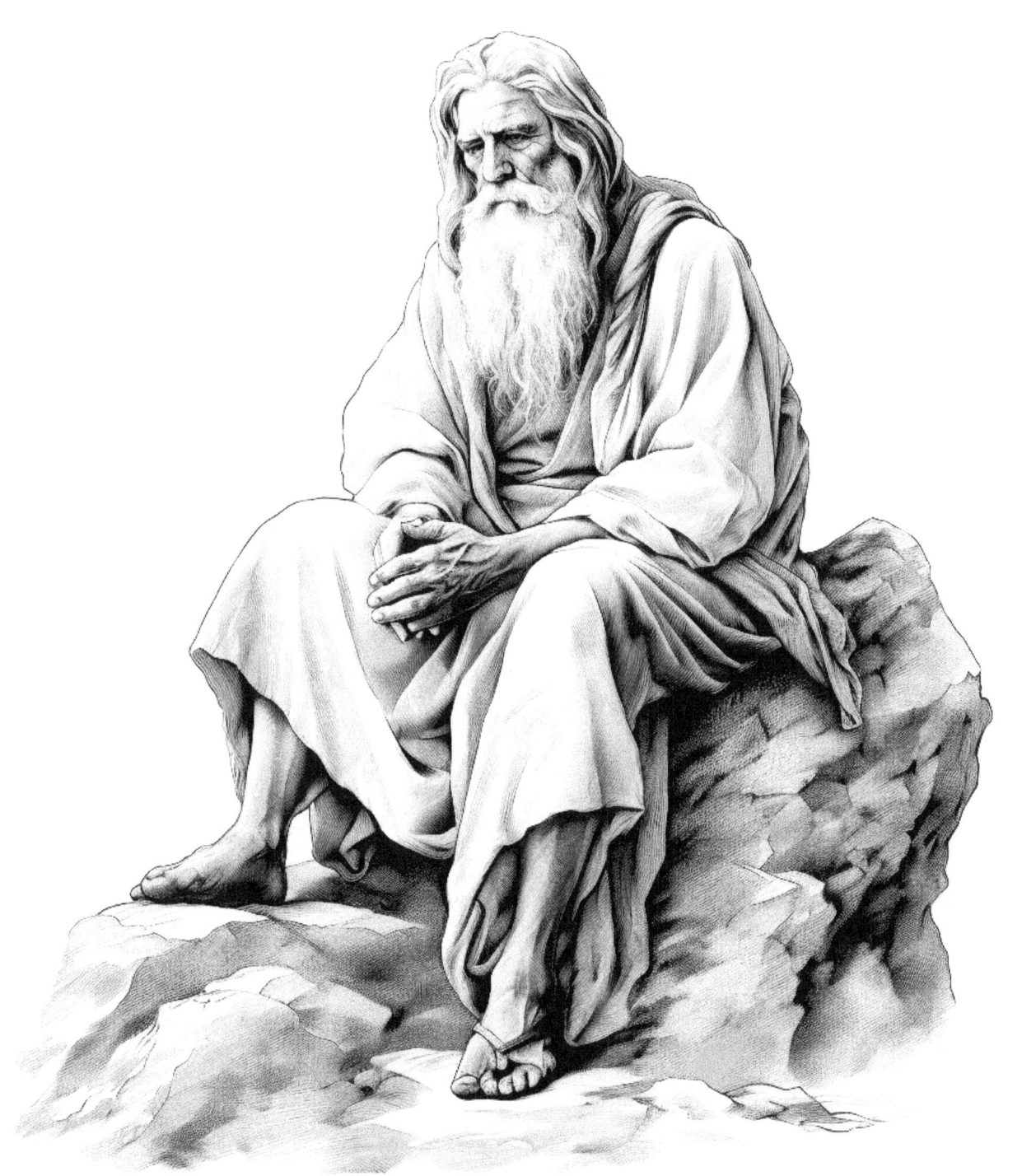

Jeremiah 1:5 "Before I formed you in the womb I knew you, before you were born I set you apart; I appointed you as a prophet to the nations

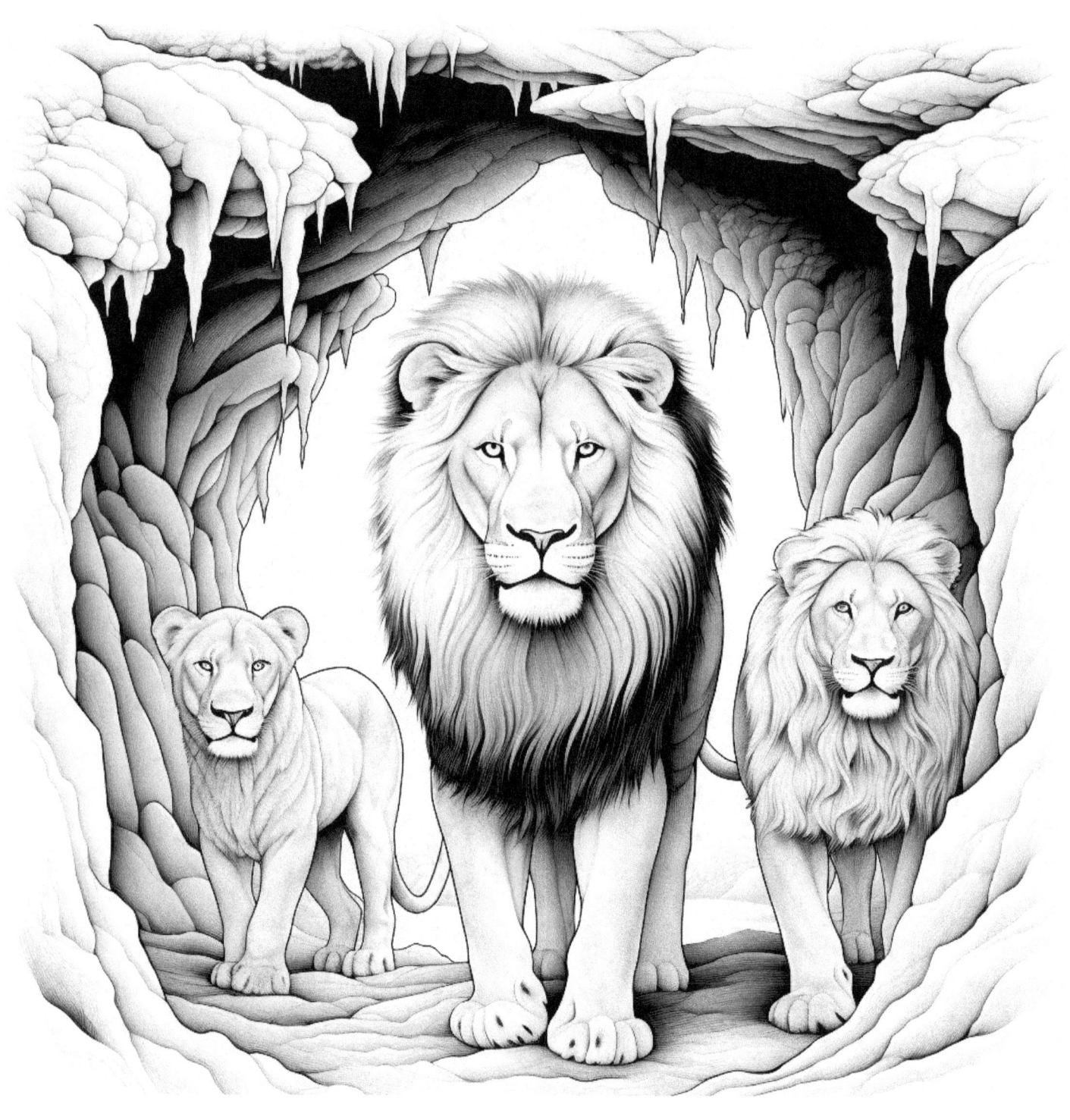

Daniel 6:26
For he is the living God and he endures
forever; his kingdom will not be destroyed,
his dominion will never end.

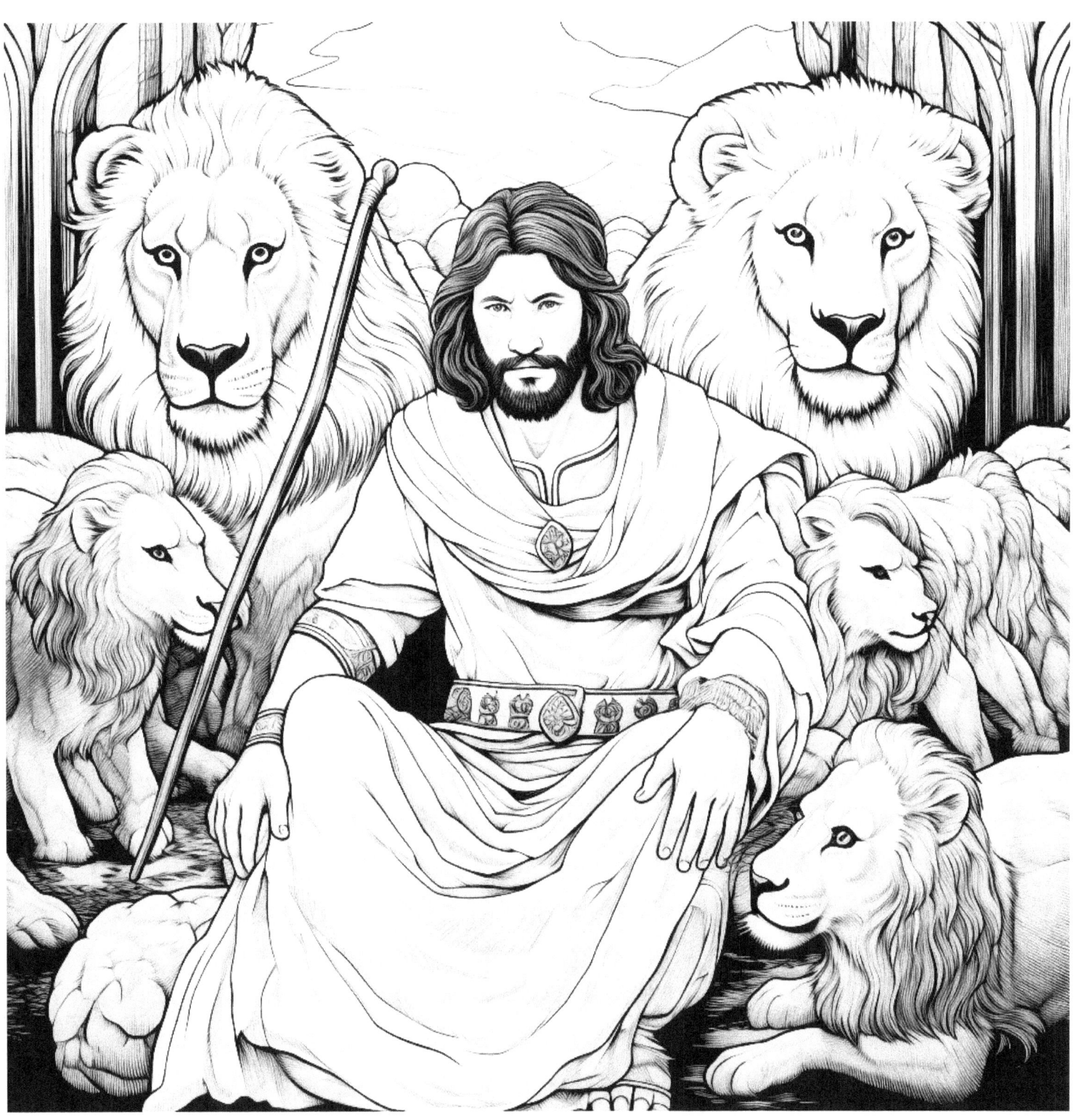

Daniel 6:27

He rescues and he saves; he performs signs and
wonders in the heavens and on the earth. He
has rescued Daniel from the power of the lions."

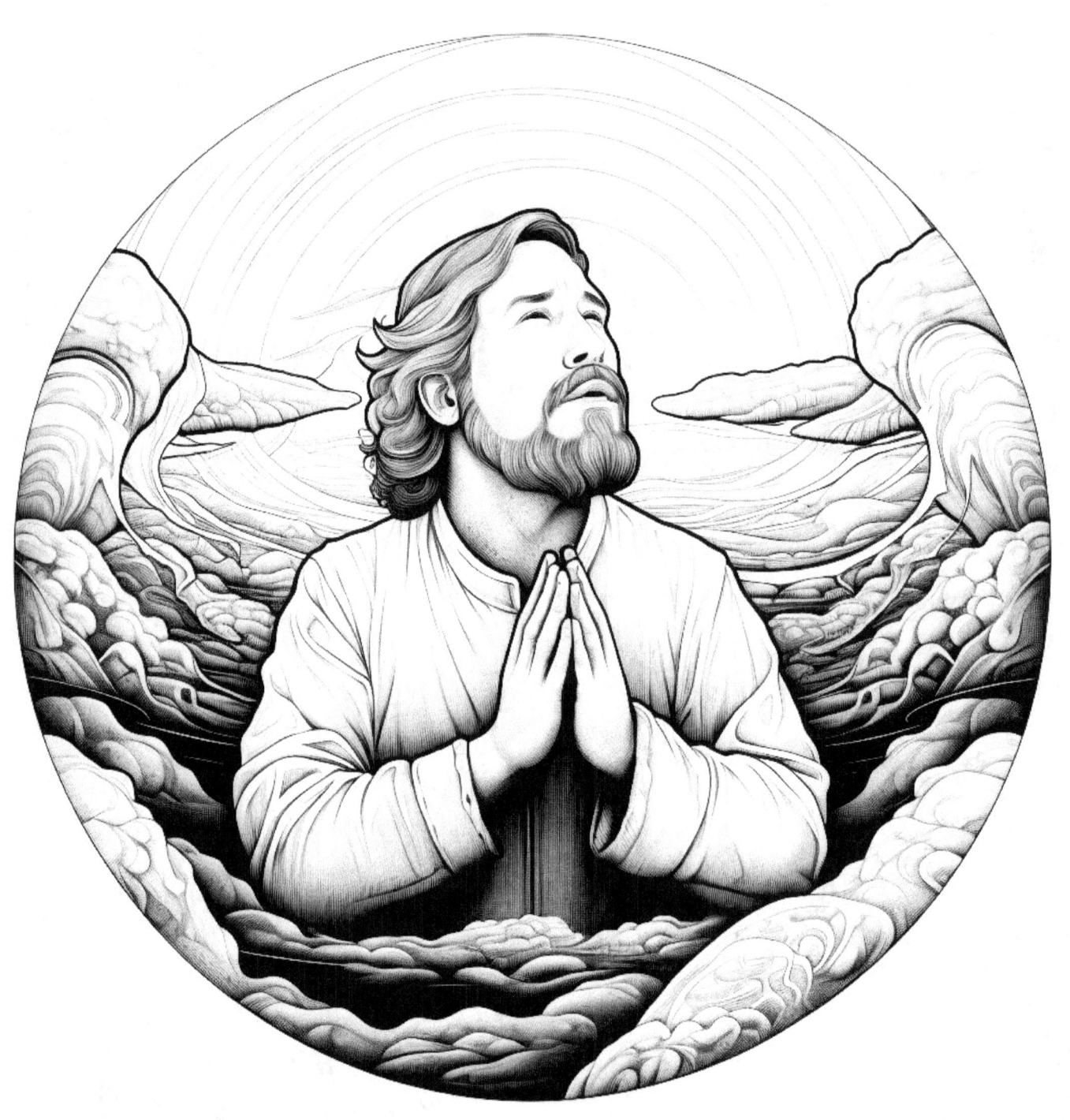

Jonah 2:1 From inside the fish Jonah prayed to the Lord his God. 2 He said: "In my distress I called to the Lord, and he answered me.

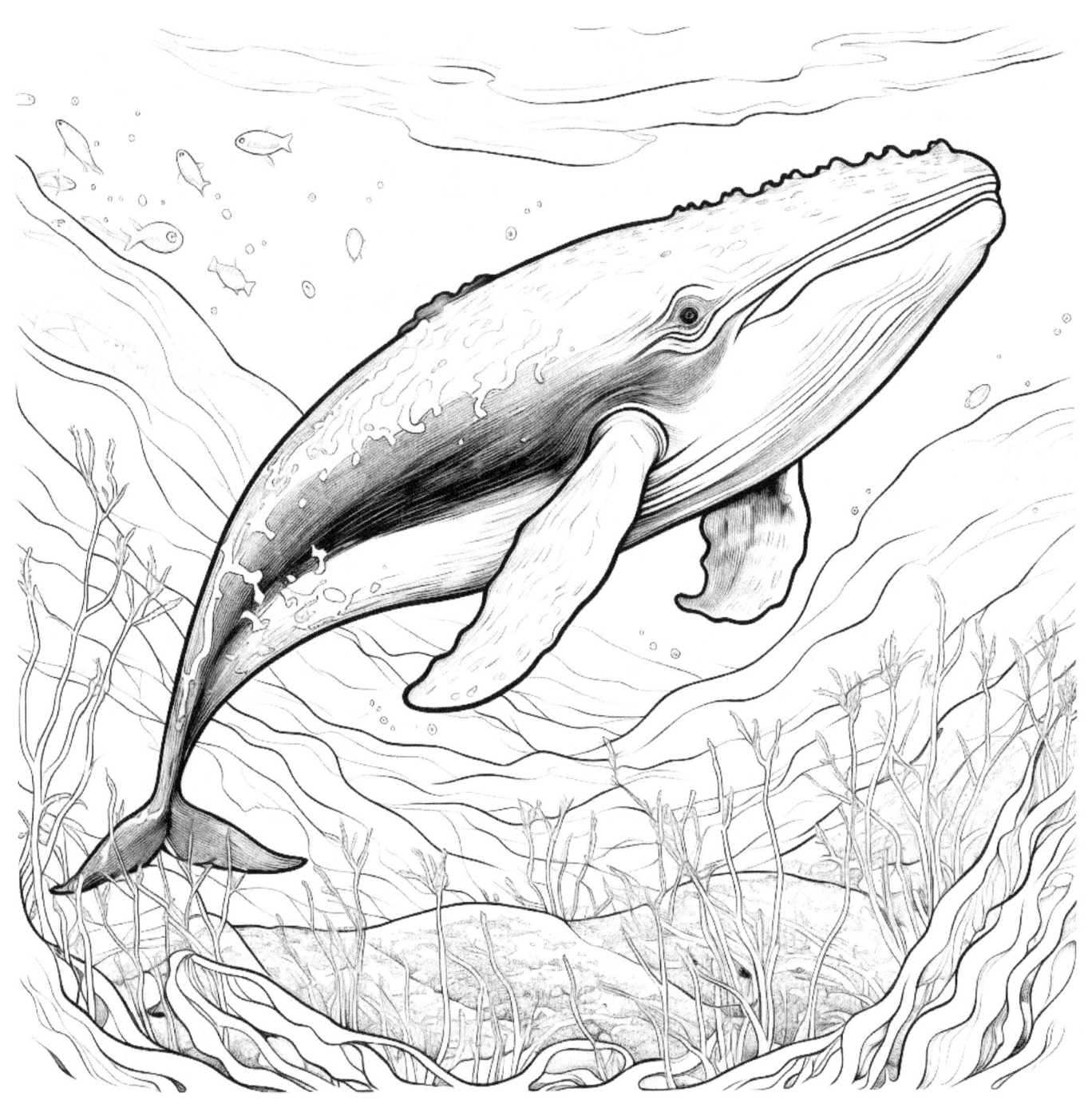

Jonah 2:1 Cont.   From deep in the
realm of the dead I called for help,
and you listened to my cry.

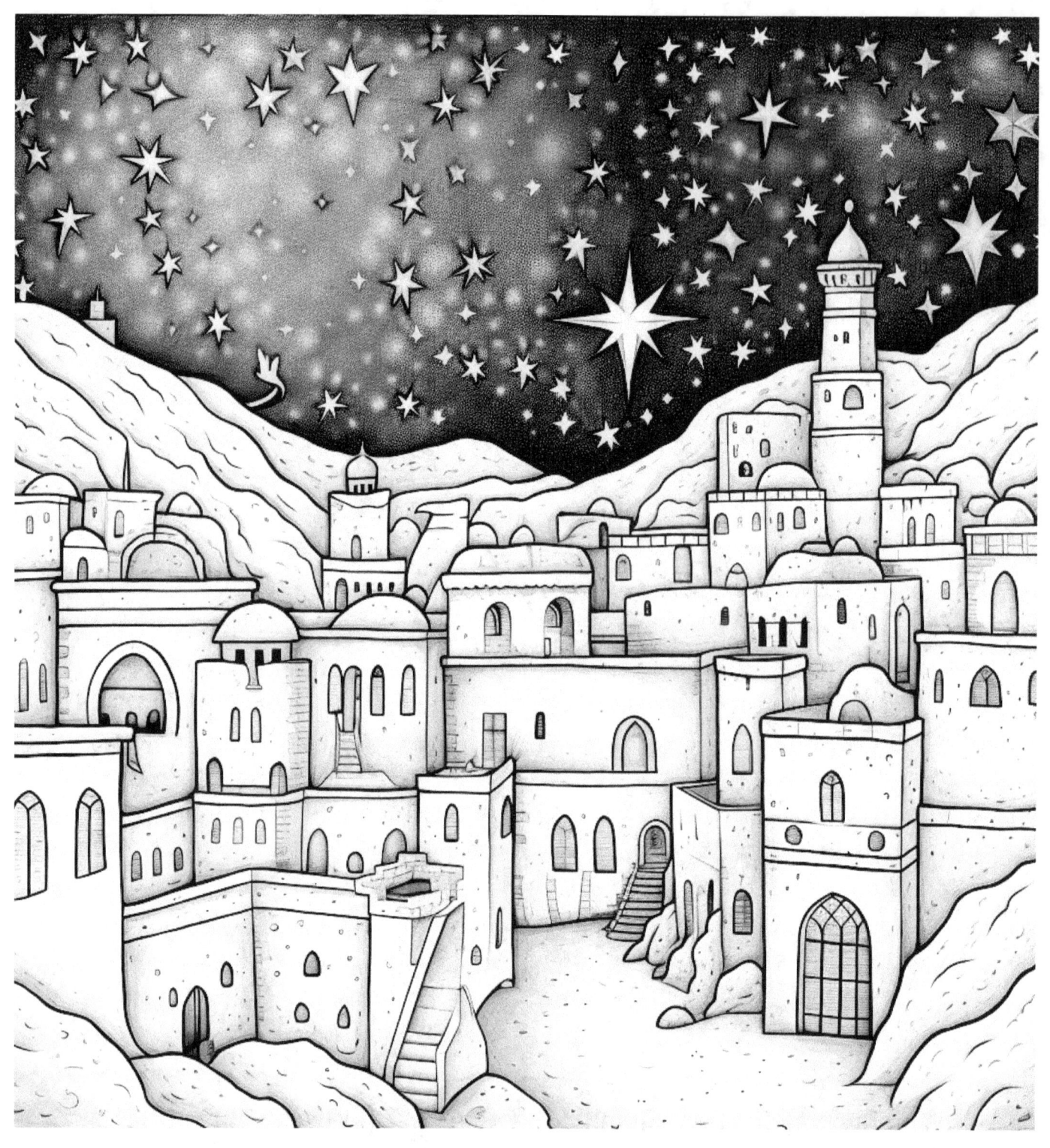

Luke 2:11 Today in the town of David a Savior has been born to you; he is the Messiah, the Lord.

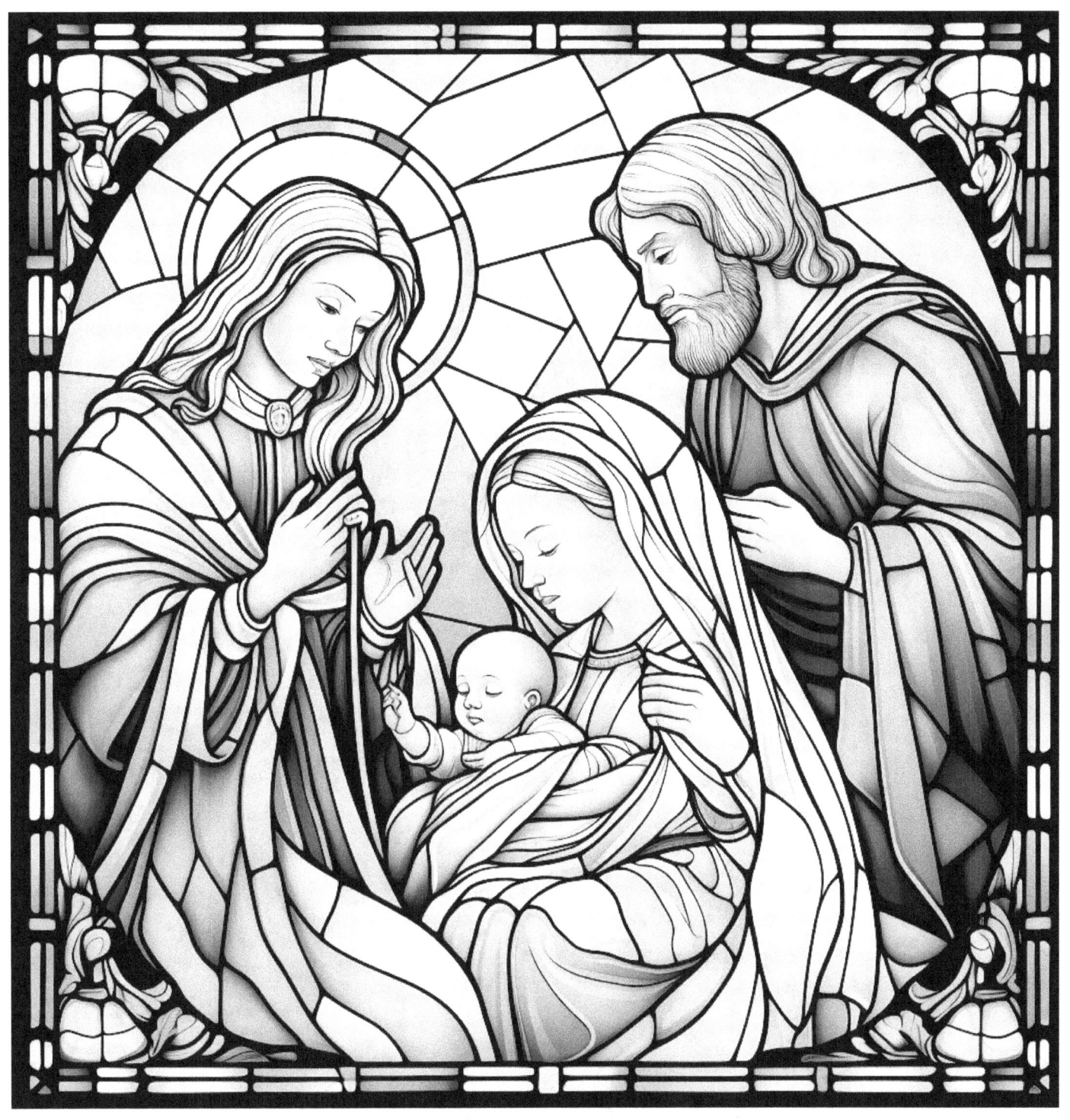

Luke 2:12 This will be a sign to you: You will find a baby wrapped in cloths and lying in a manger."

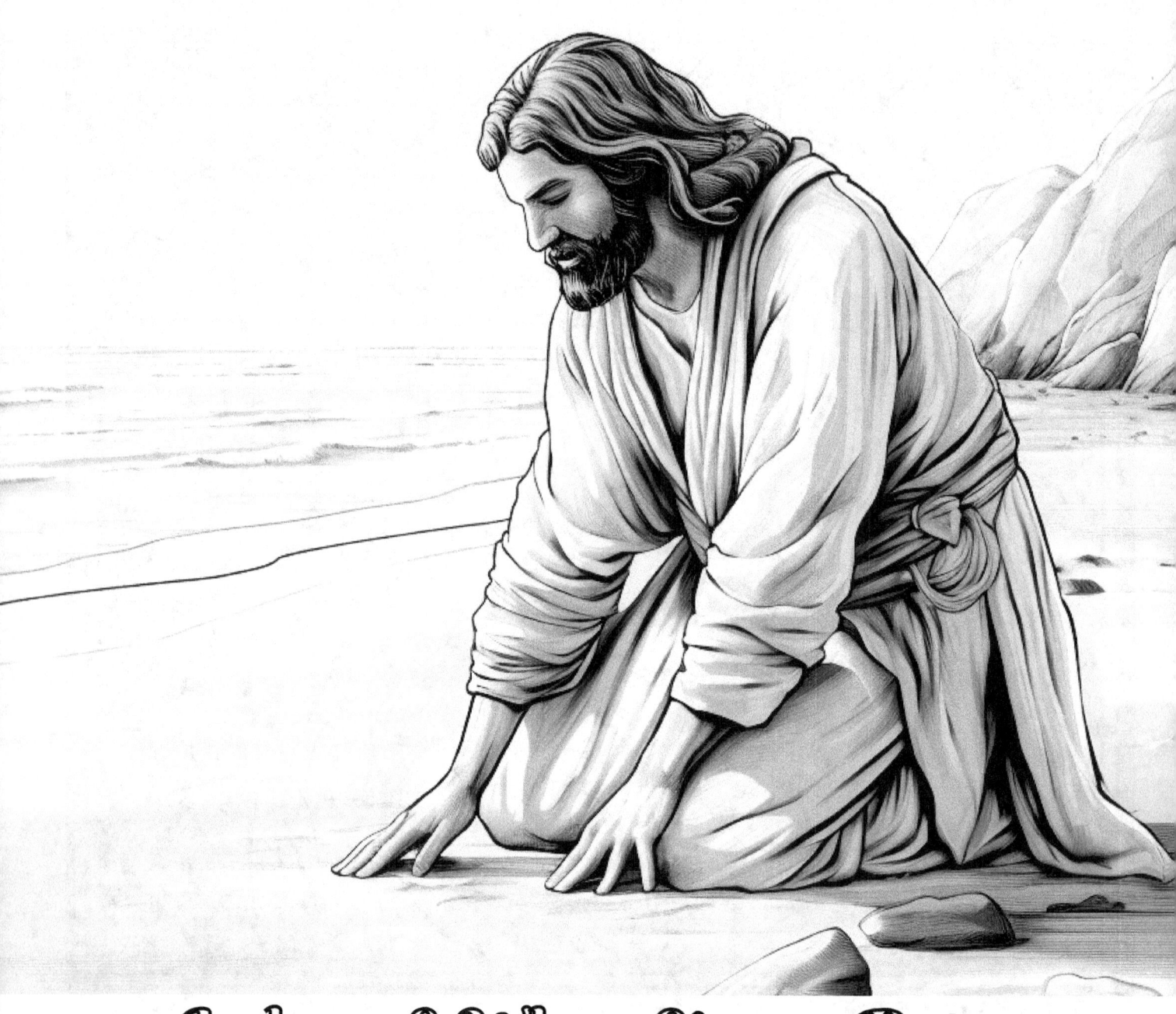

Luke 5:8 When Simon Peter saw this, he fell at Jesus' knees and said, "Go away from me, Lord; I am a sinful man!"

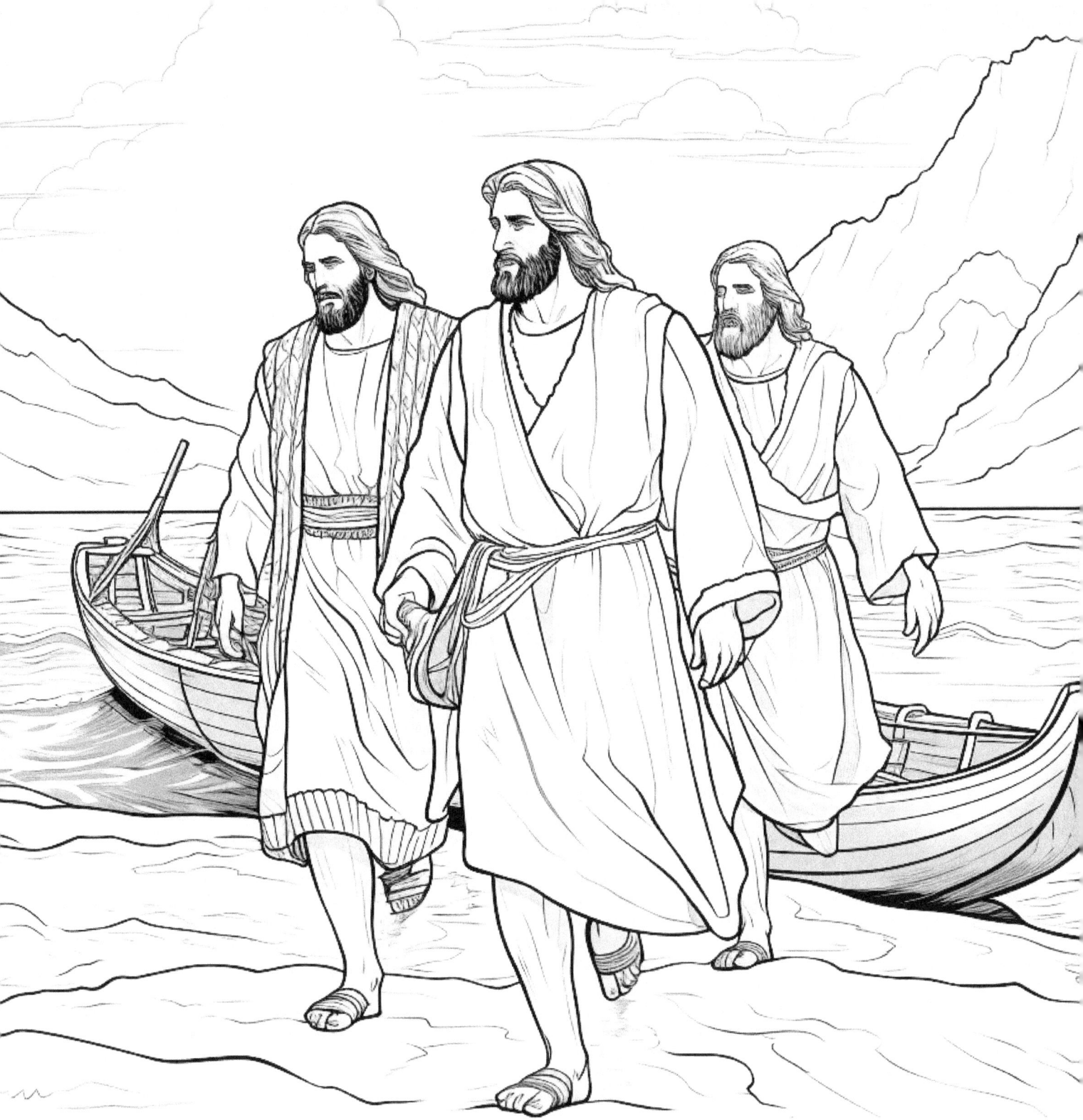

Luke 5:10...Then Jesus said to Simon, "Don't be afraid; from now on you will fish for people." 11 So they pulled their boats up on shore, left everything and followed him.

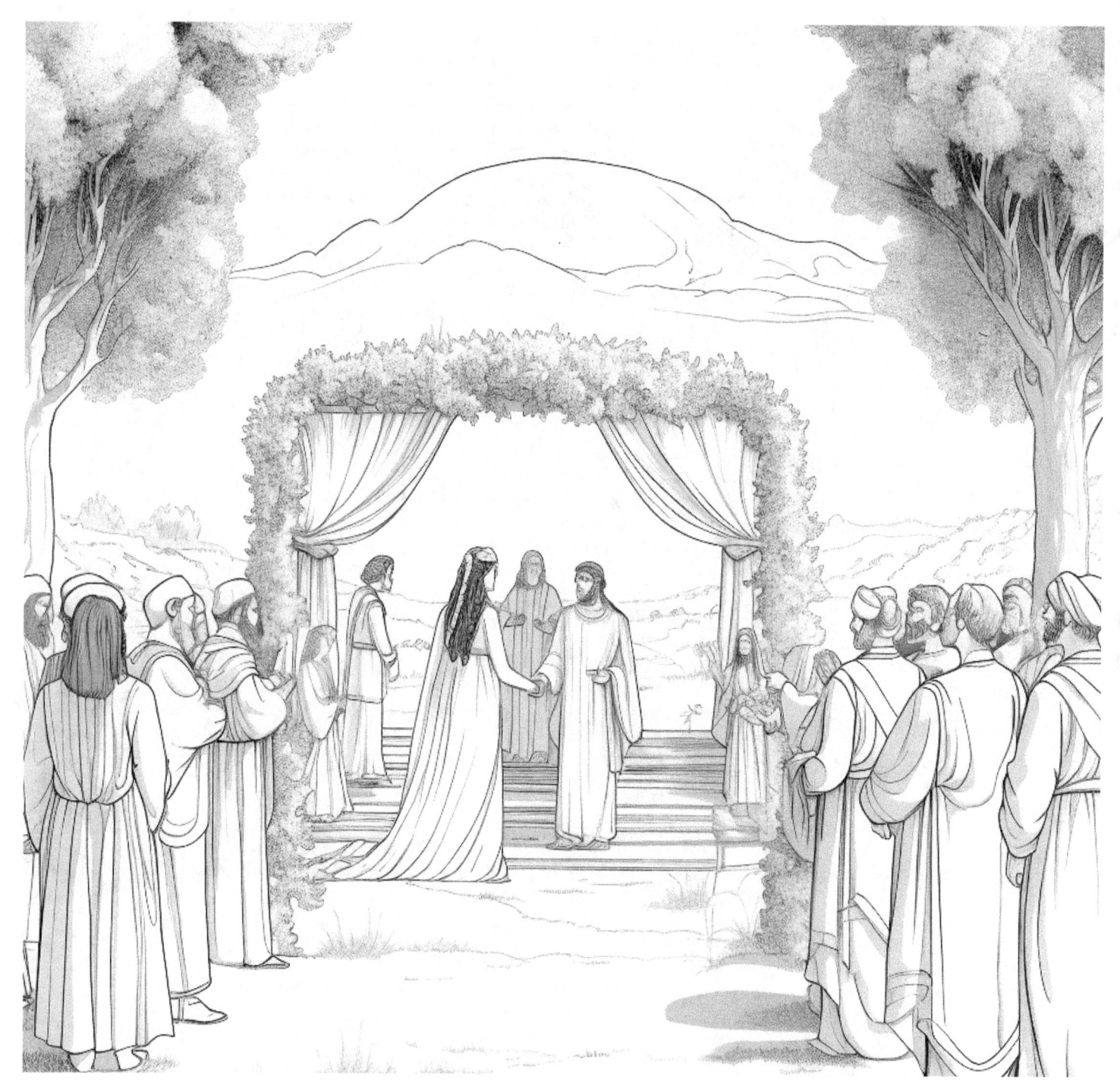

John 2:10...but you have saved
the best till now."

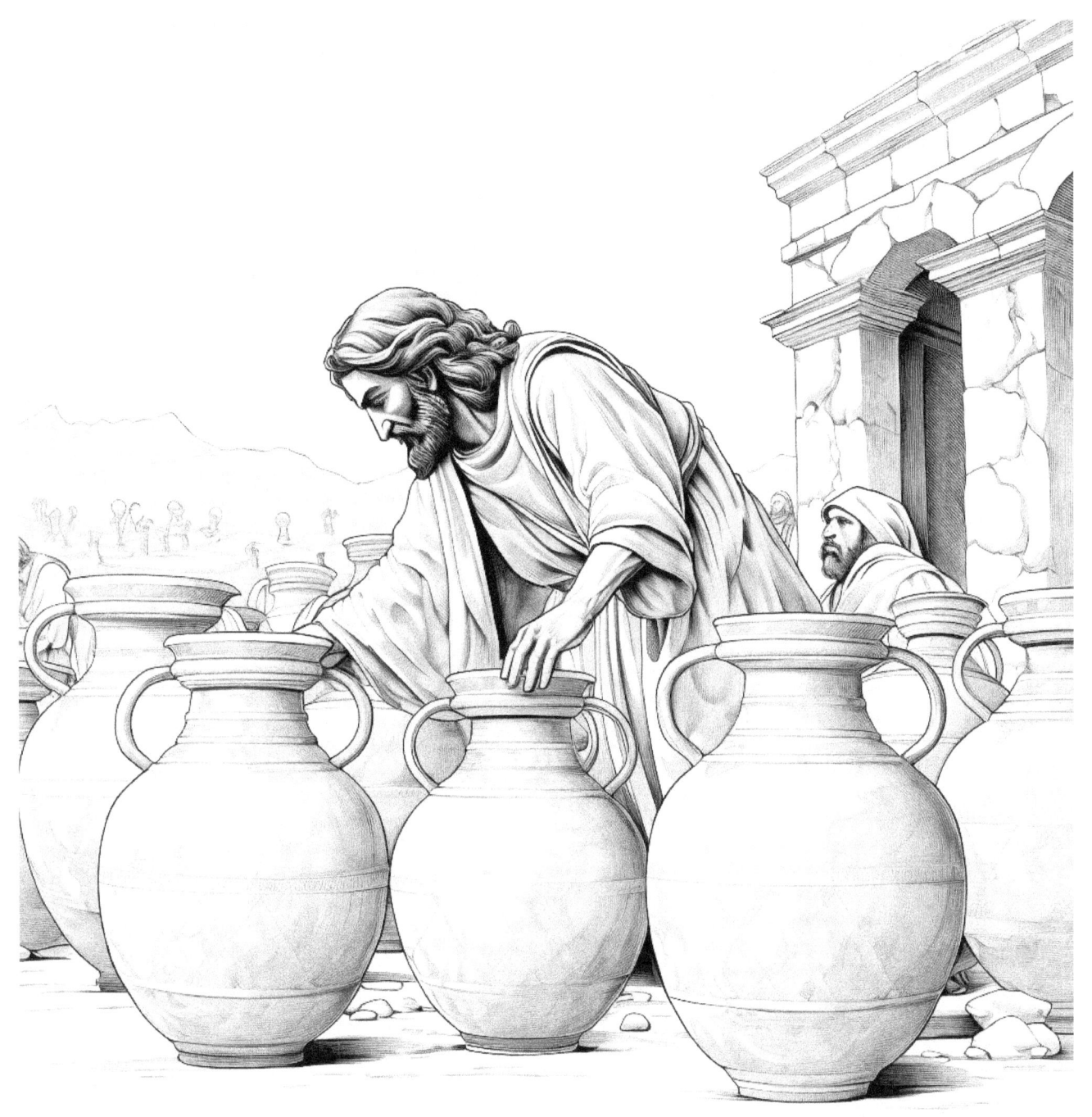

John 2:11 What Jesus did here in Cana of Galilee was the first of the signs through which he revealed his glory; and his disciples believed in him.

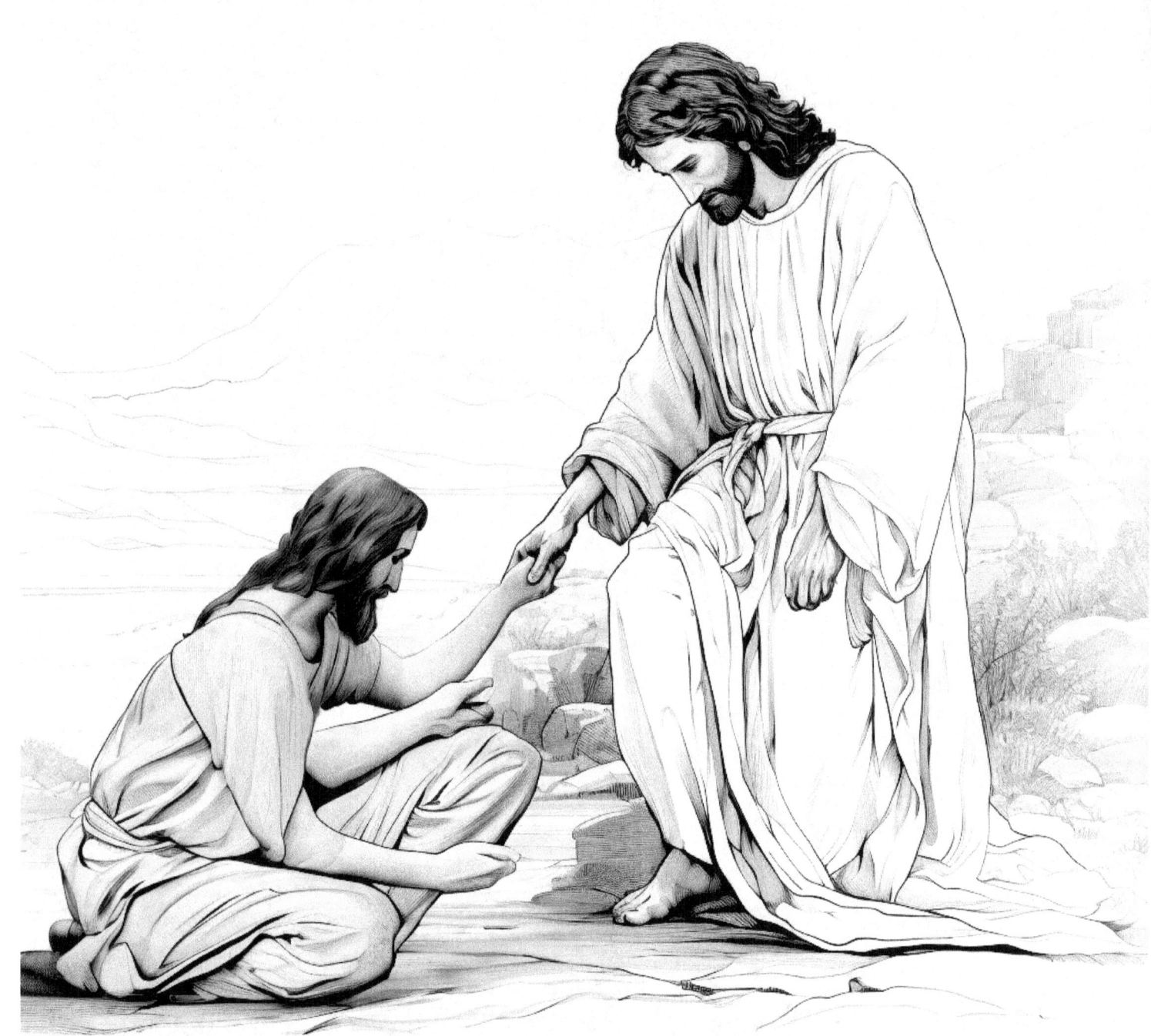

John 4:50 Jesus said to him, "Go your way; your son lives." So the man believed the word that Jesus spoke to him, and he went his way.

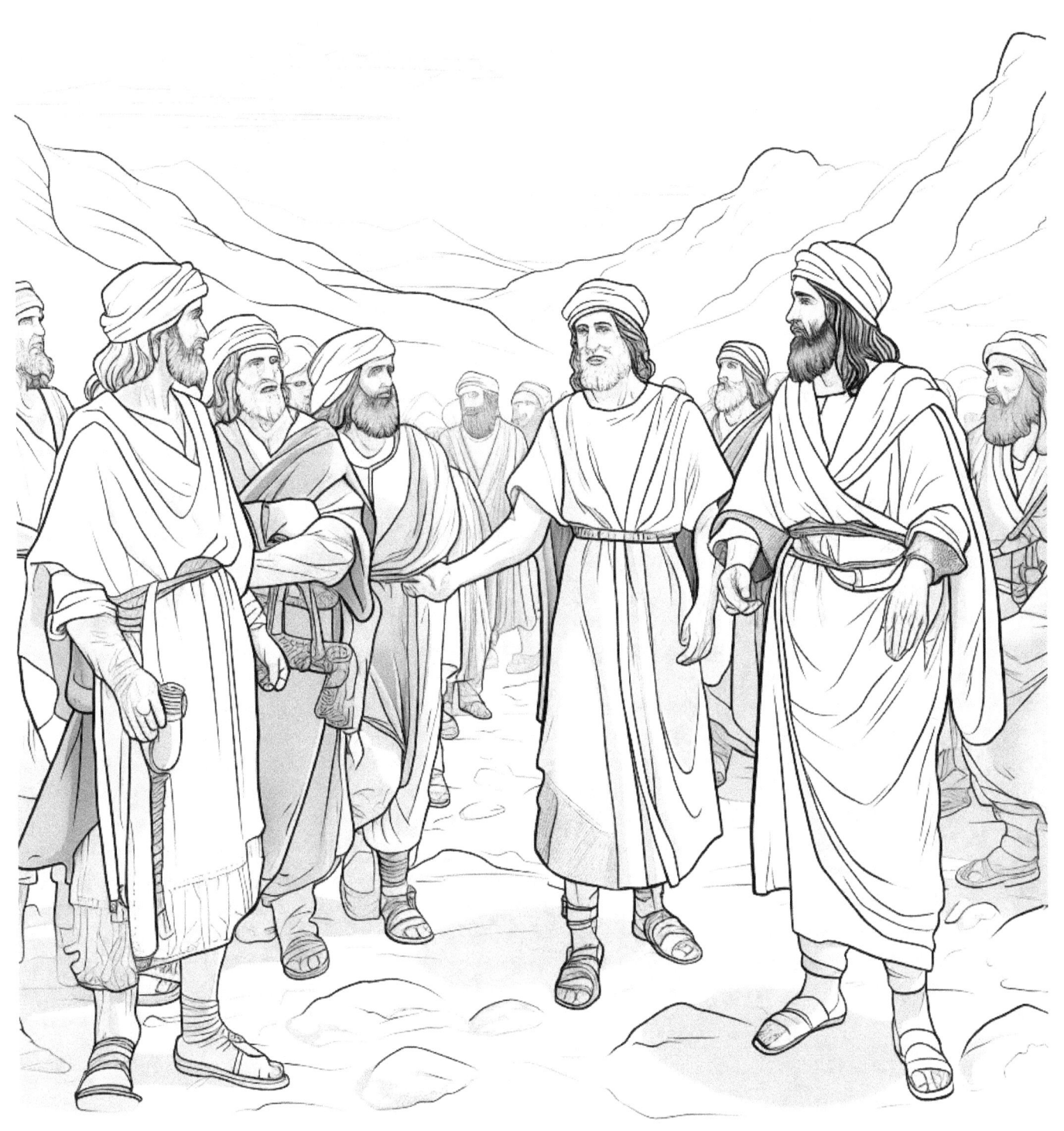

John 4:51 And as he was now going down, his servants met him and told him, saying, "Your son lives!"

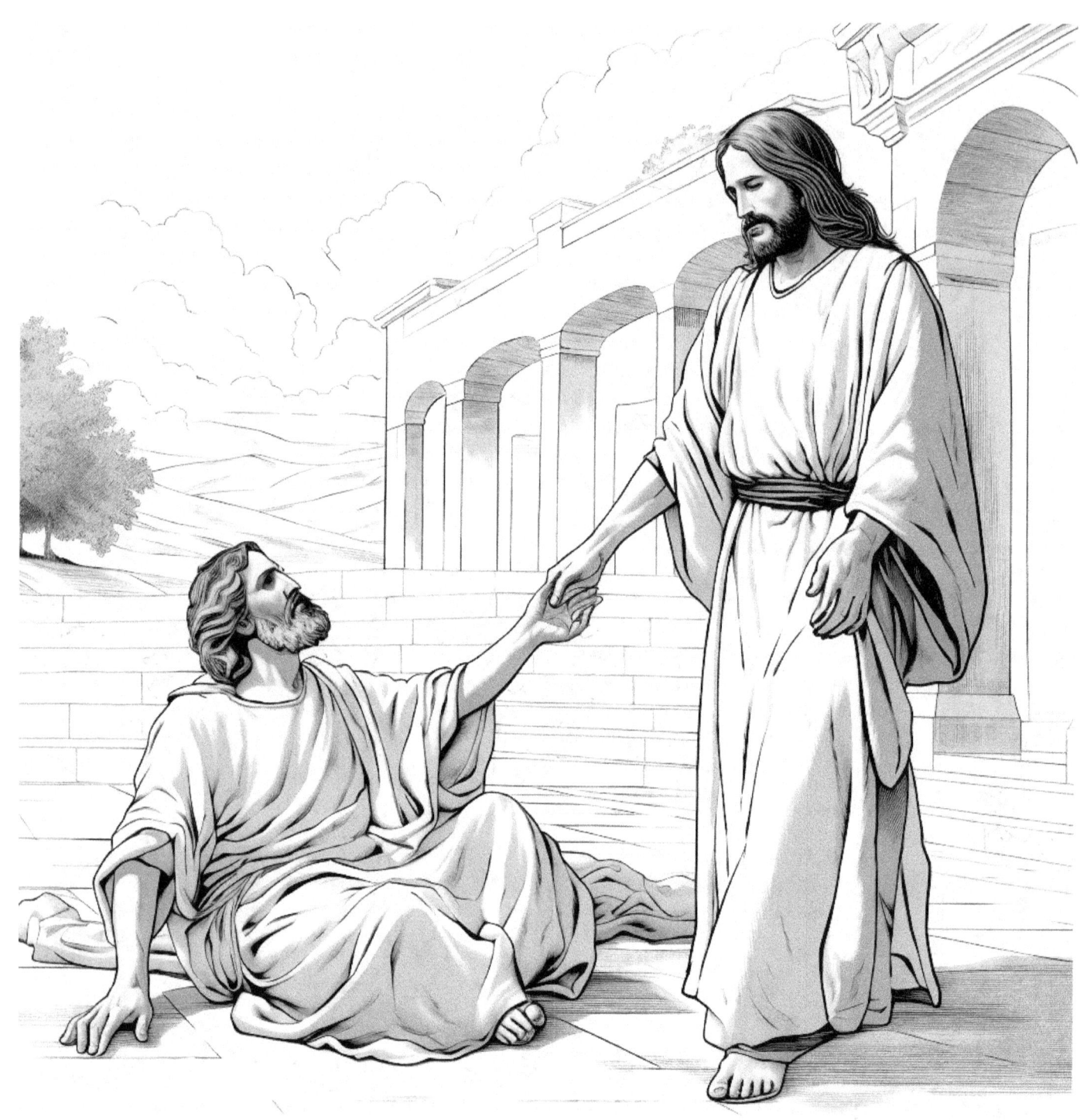

John 5:6 When Jesus saw him lying there and learned that he had been in this condition for along time, he asked him, "Do you want to get well?"

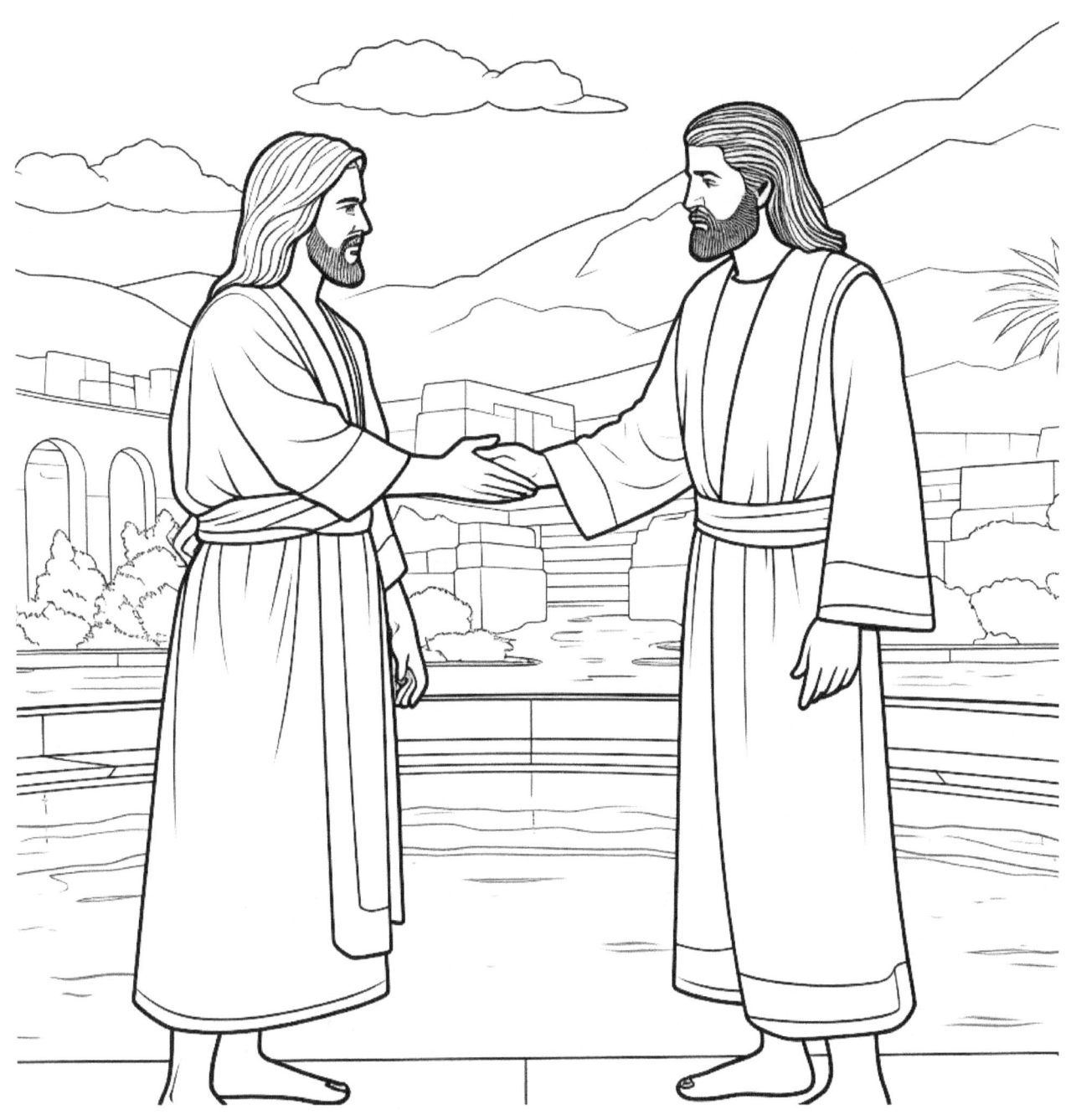

John 5:8 Then Jesus said to him, "Get up! Pick up your mat and walk." 9 At once the man was cured; he picked up his mat and walked.

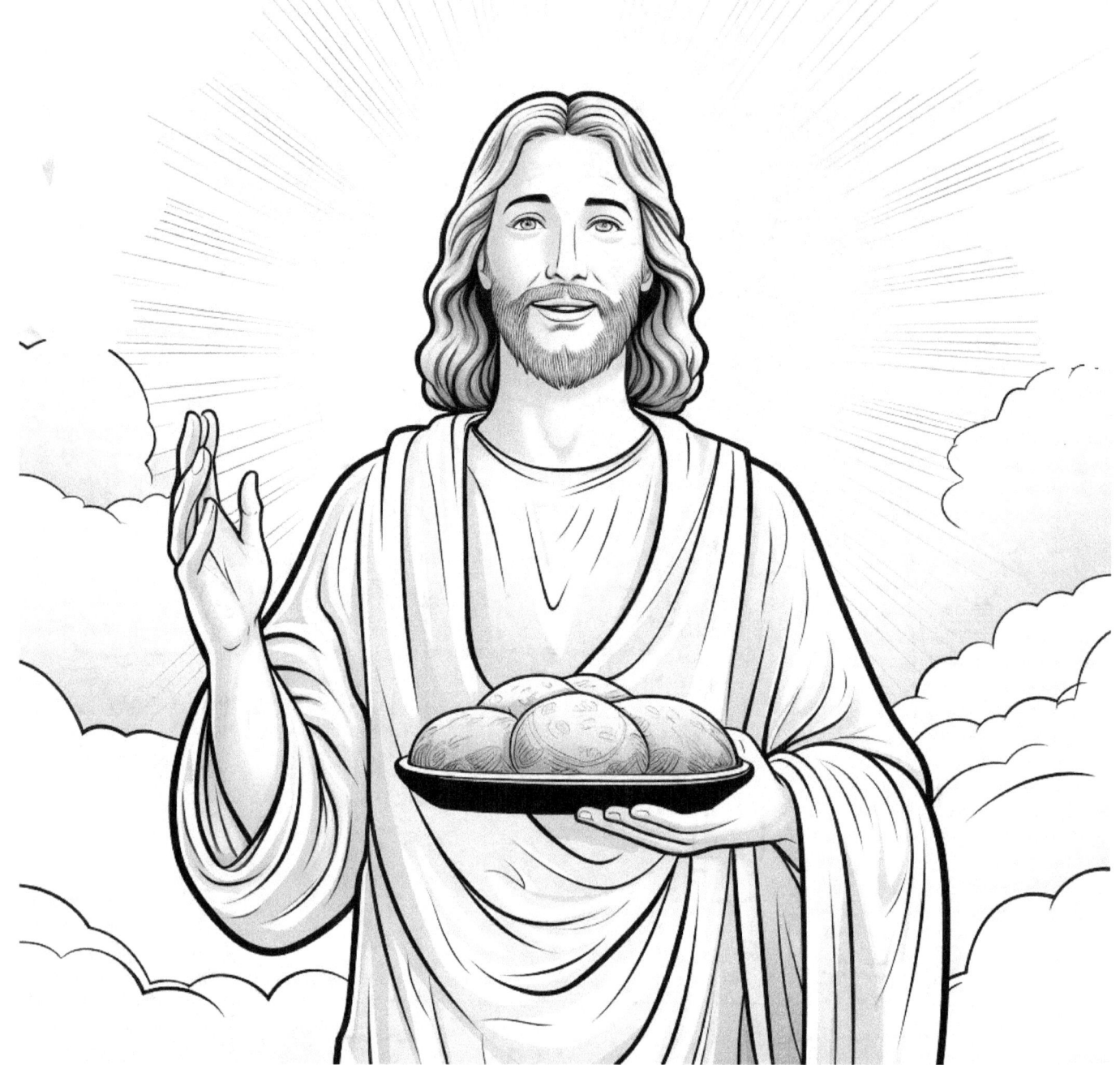

Luke 9:16 Taking the five loaves and the two fish and looking up to heaven, he gave thanks and broke them. Then he gave them to the disciples to distribute to the people.

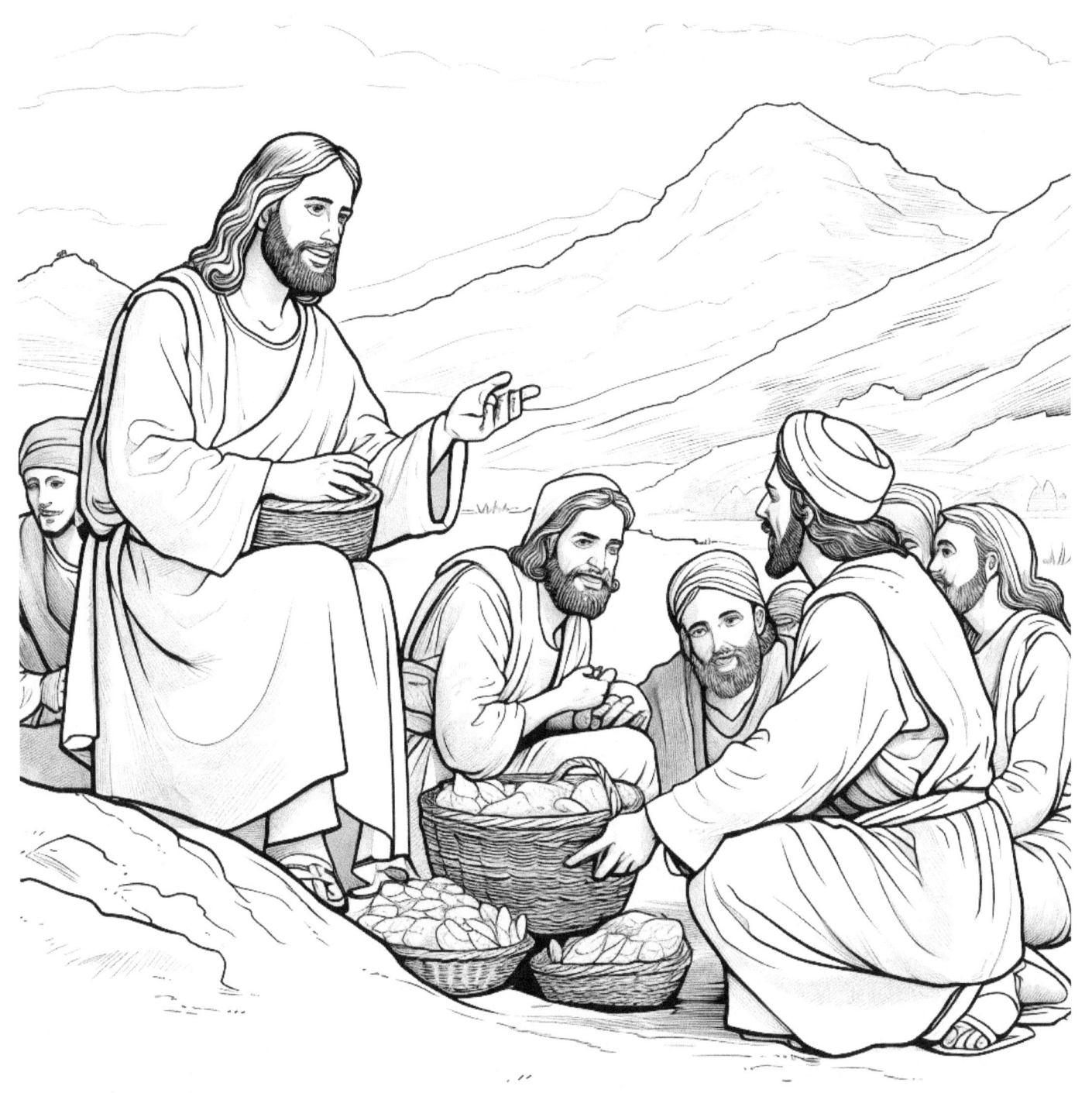

17 They all ate and were satisfied, and the disciples picked up twelve basketfuls of broken pieces that were left over.

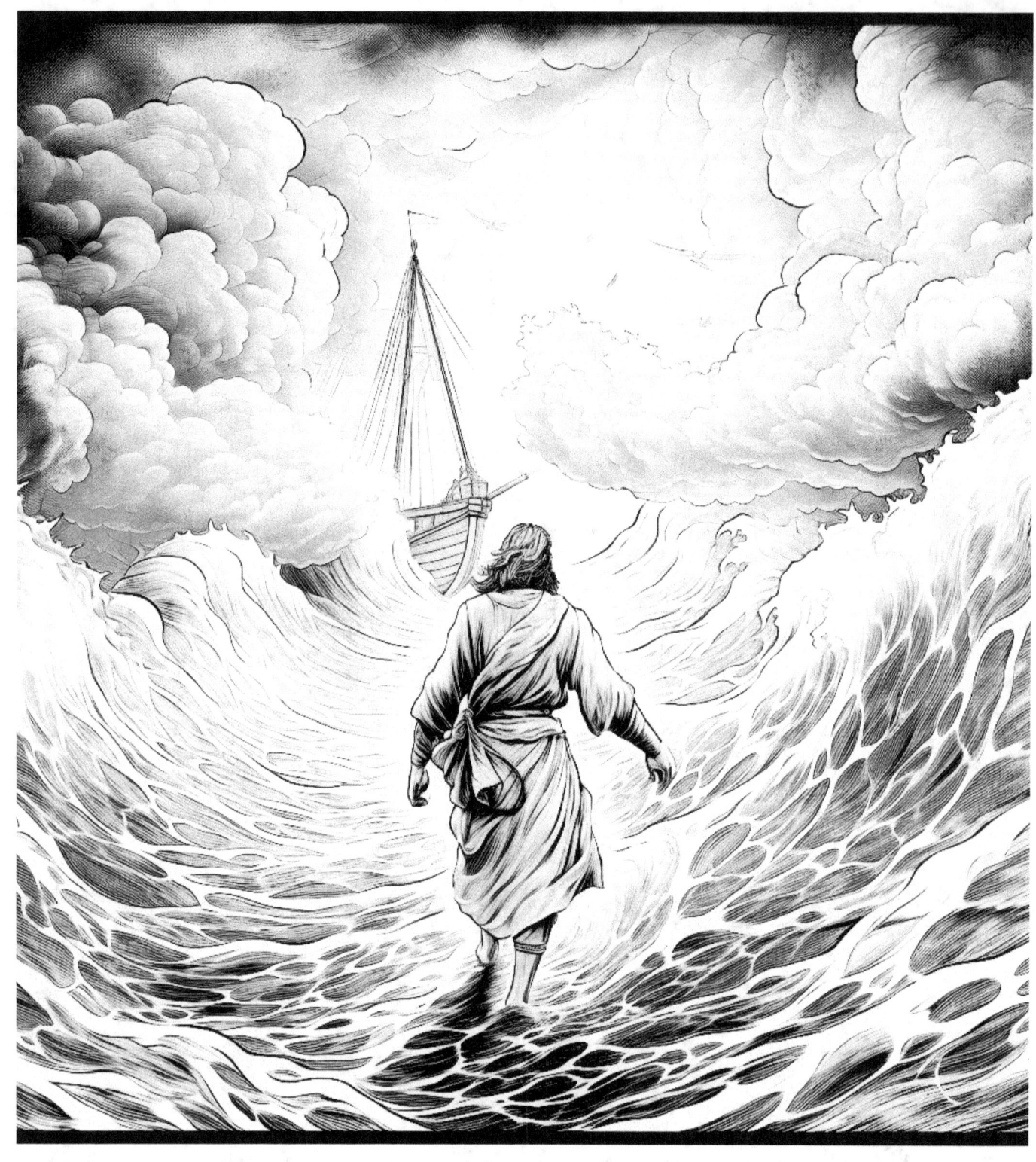

Matthew 14:27 But Jesus immediately said to them: "Take courage! It is I. Don't be afraid."

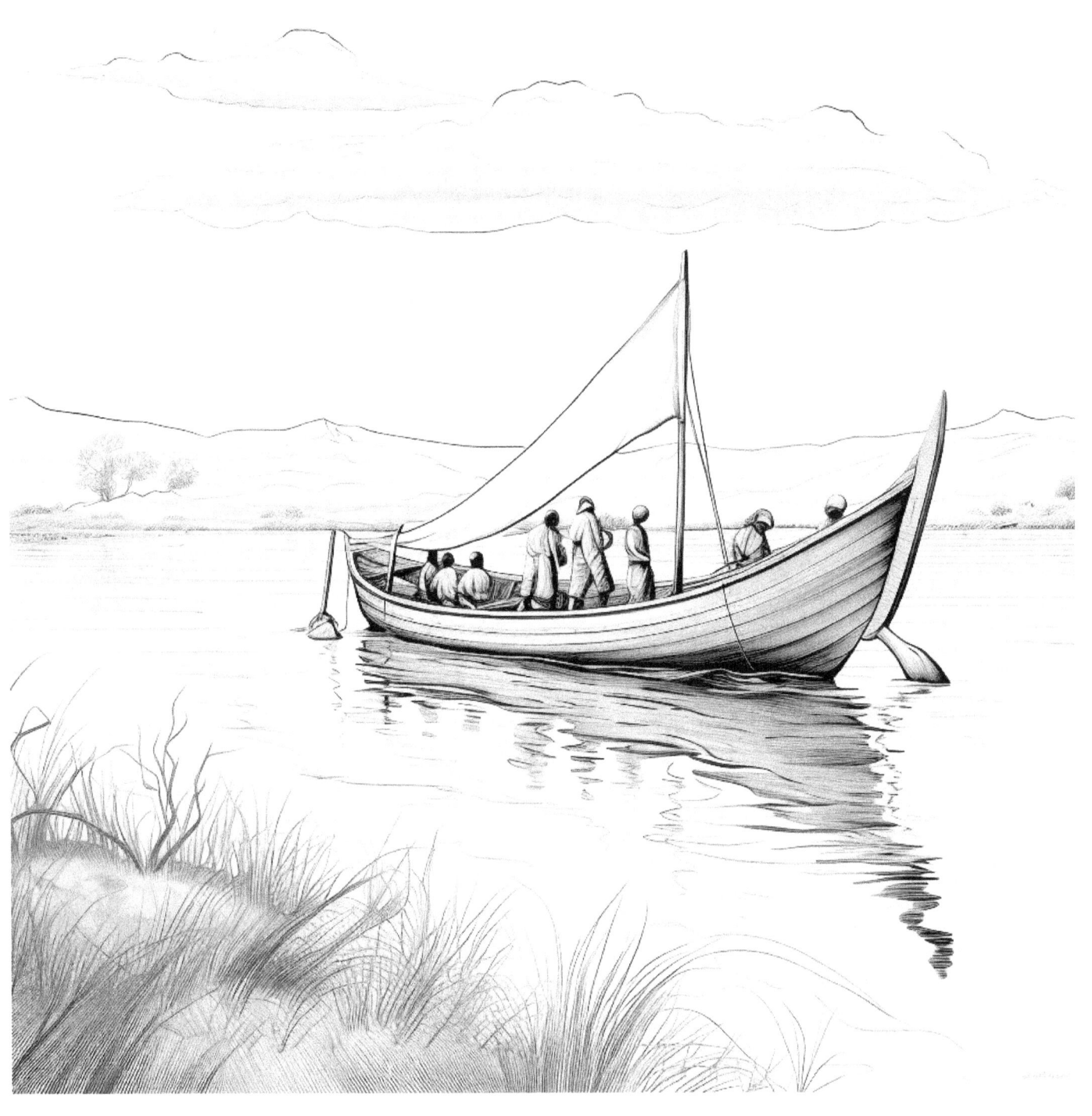

Matthew 14:32 And when they climbed into the boat, the wind died down. 33 Then those who were in the boat worshiped him, saying, "Truly you are the Son of God."

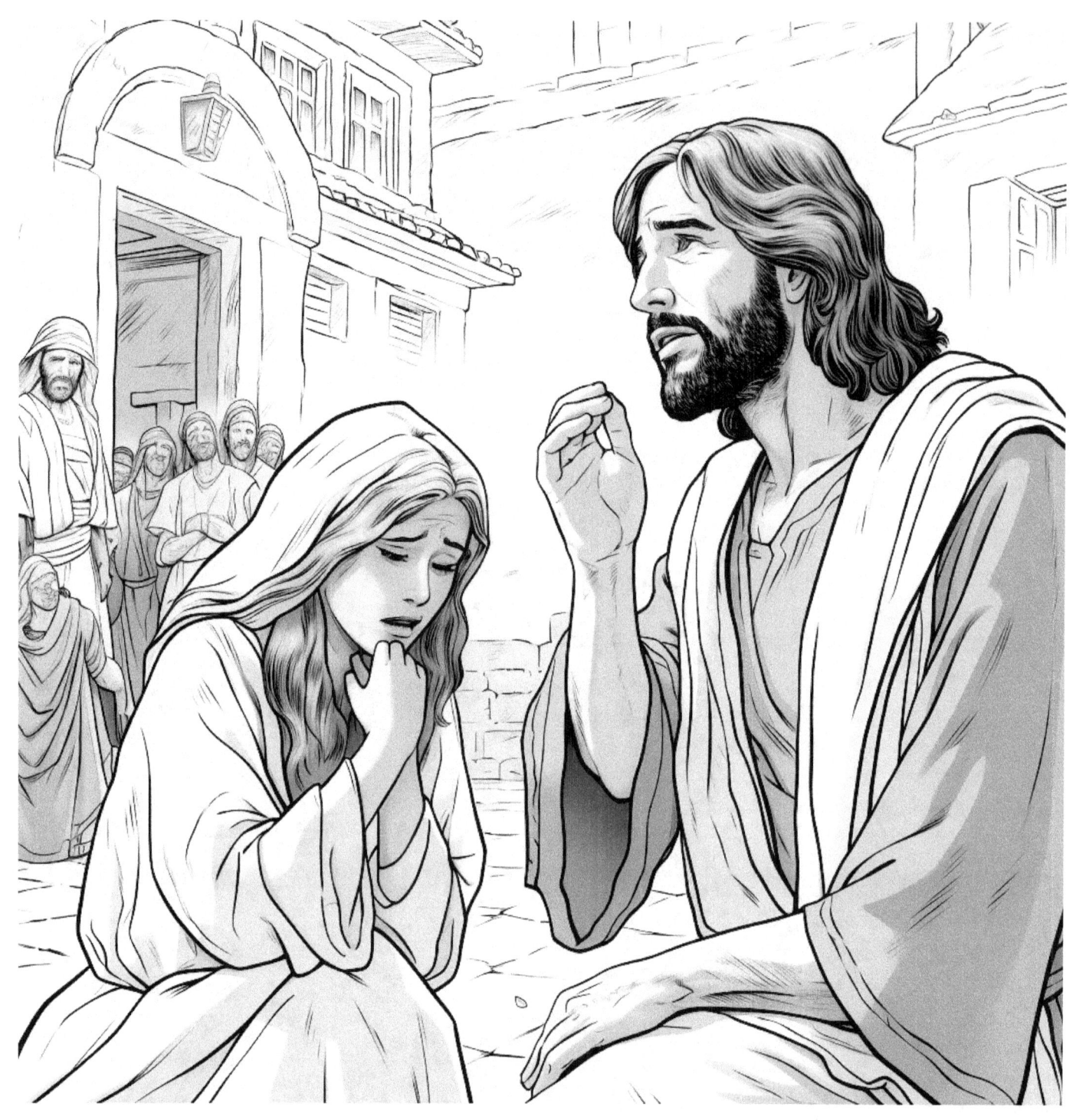

Matthew 15:22 A Canaanite woman from that vicinity came to him, crying out, "Lord, Son of David, have mercy on me! My daughter is demon-possessed and suffering terribly."

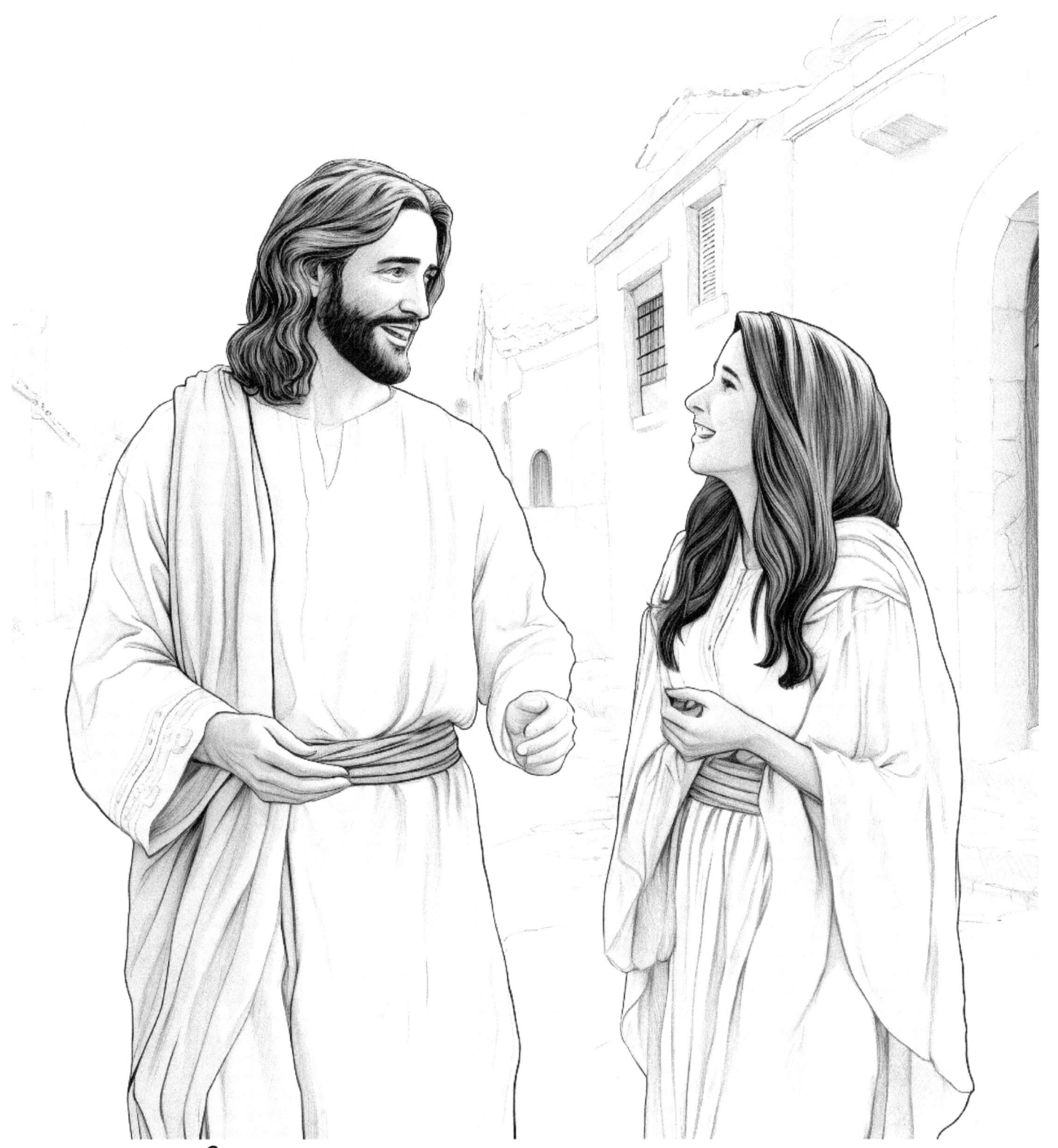

Matthew 15:28 Then Jesus said to her, "Woman, you have great faith! Your request is granted." And her daughter was healed at that moment.

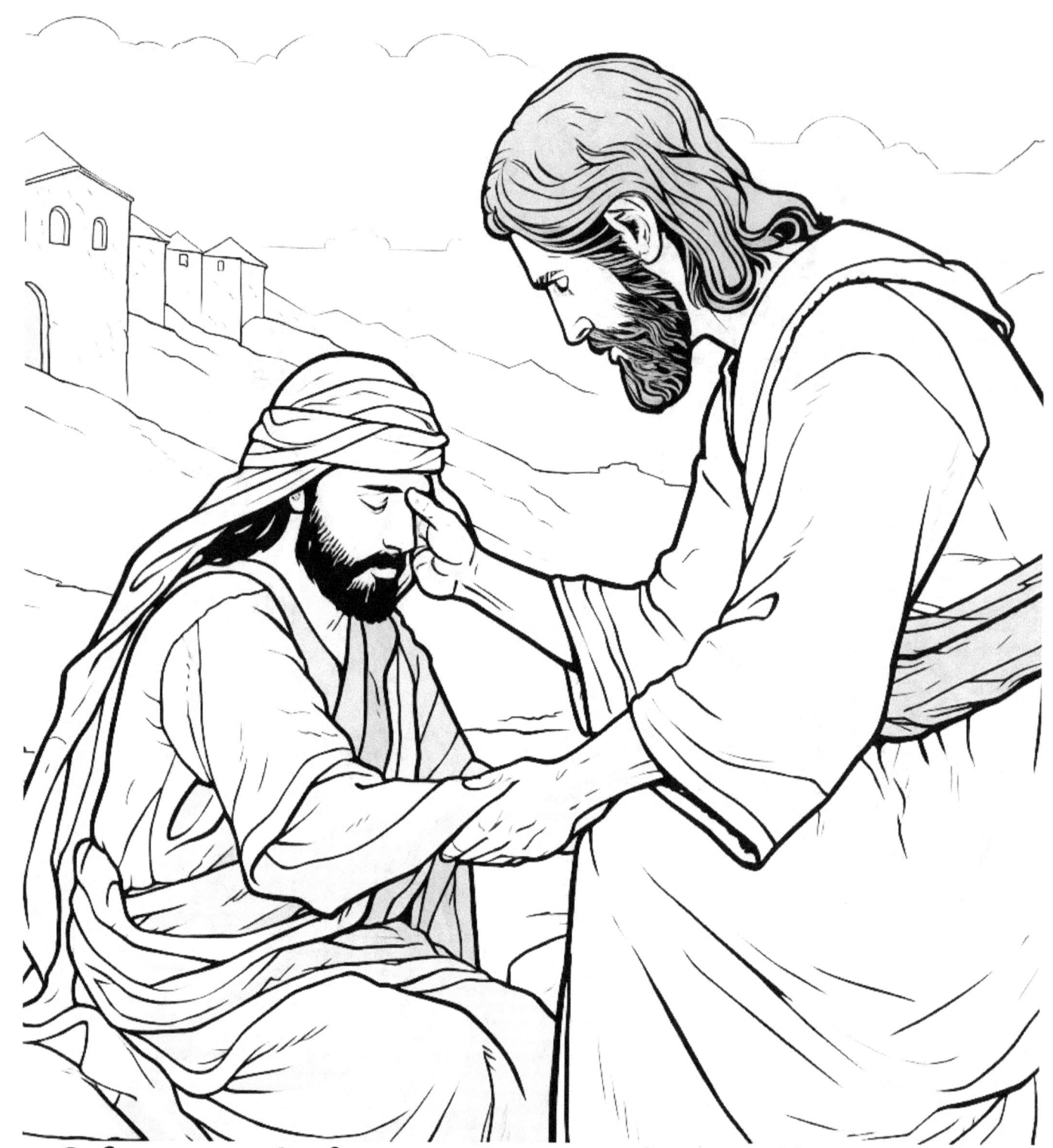

John 9:5   As long as I am in the world, I am the light of the world.   6 When he had thus spoken, he spat on the ground, and made clay of the spittle, and he anointed the eyes of the blind man with the clay,

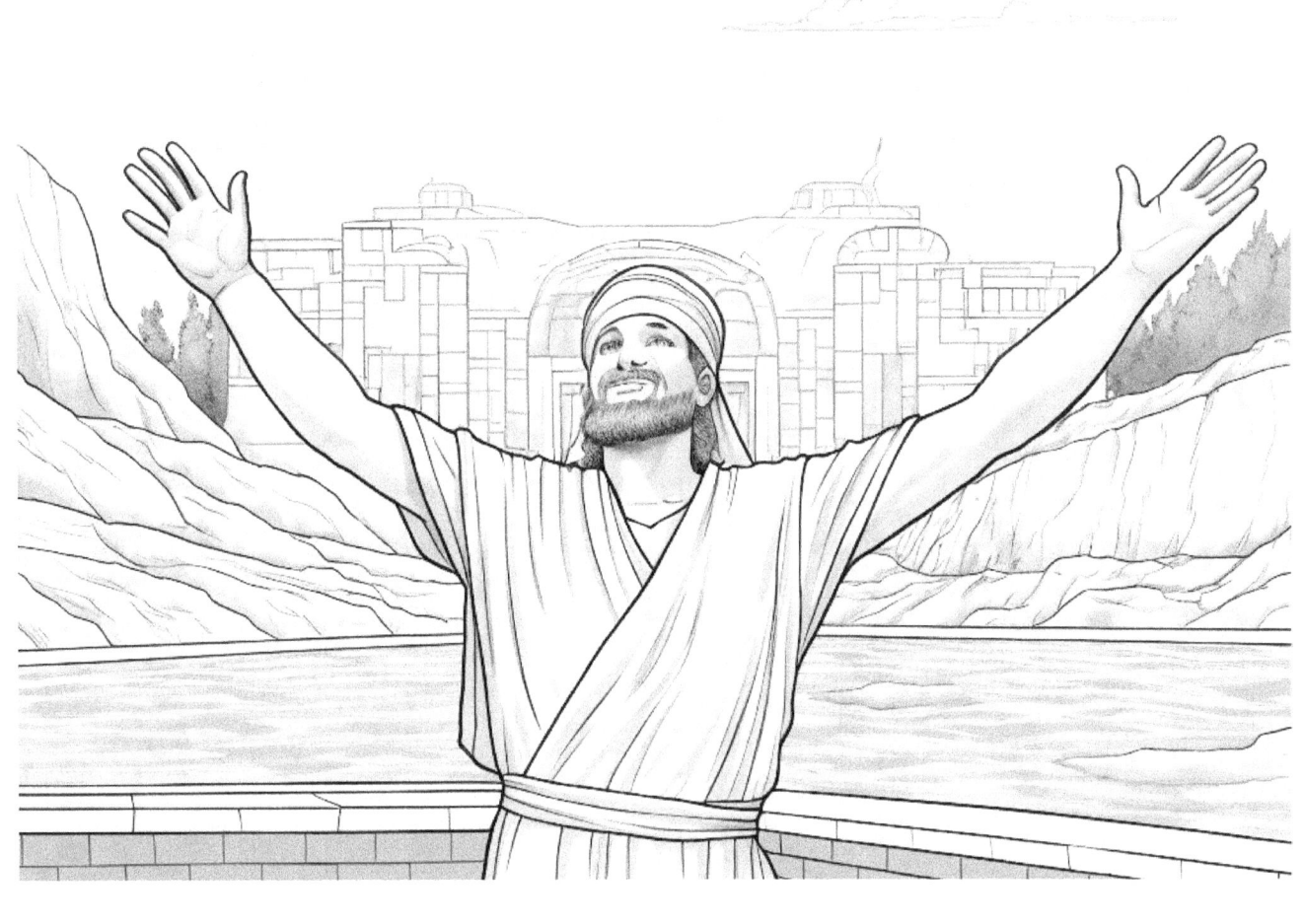

John 9:7   And said unto him, Go, wash in the pool of Siloam. He went his way therefore, and washed, and came seeing.

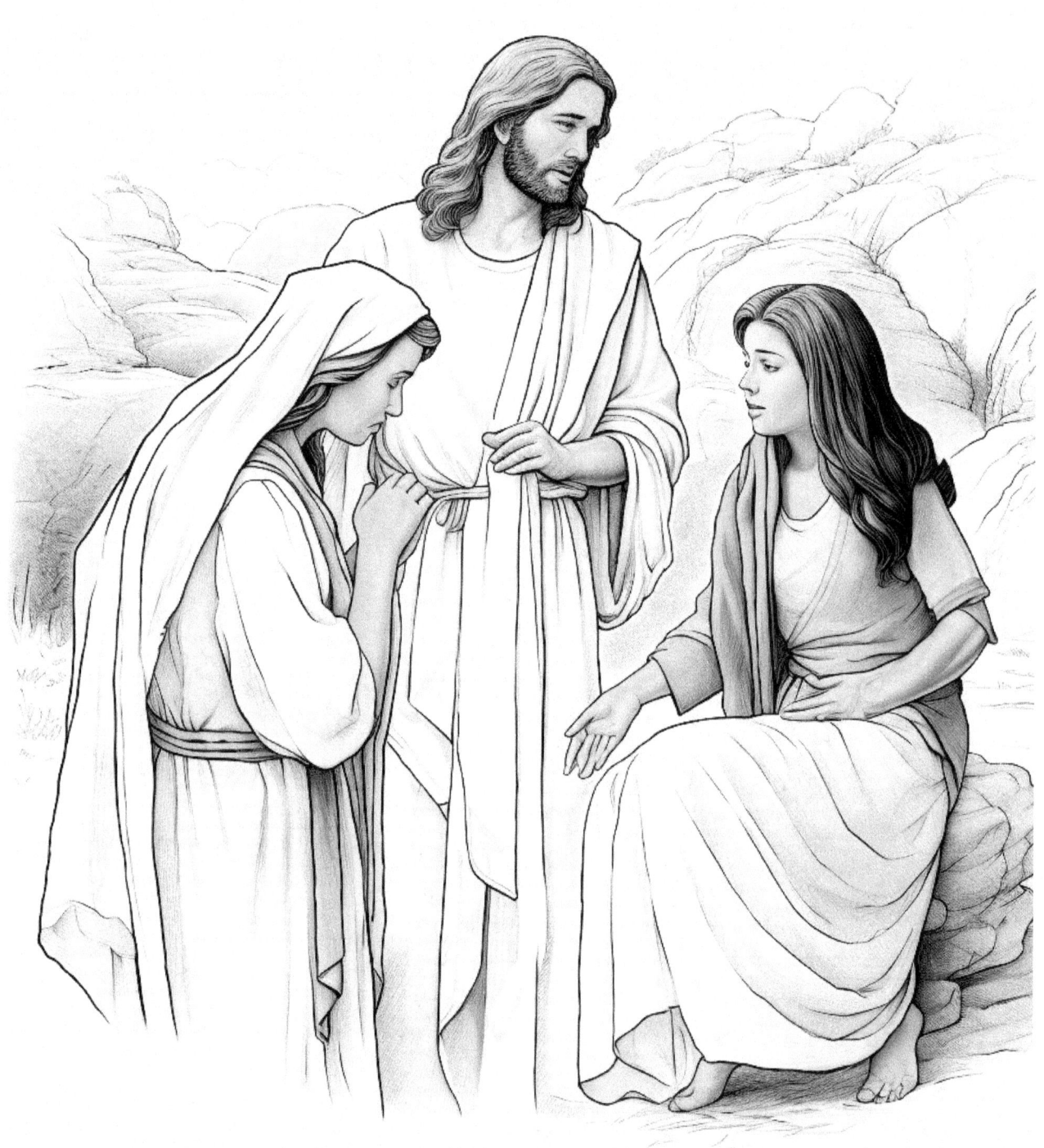

John 11:40 Jesus saith unto her, Said I not unto thee, that, if thou wouldest believe, thou shouldest see the glory of God?

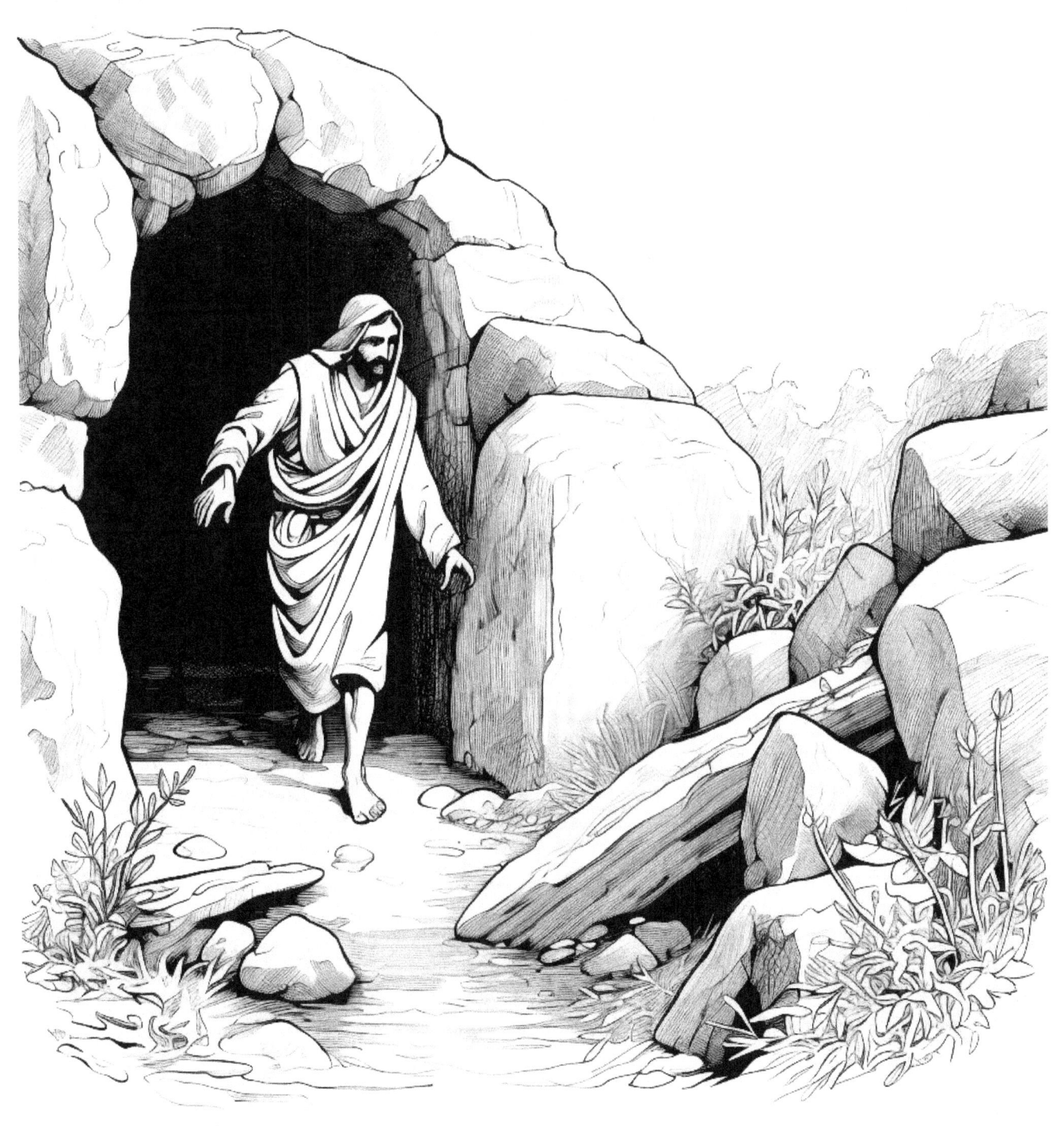

John 11:43 And when he thus had spoken, he cried with a loud voice, Lazarus, come forth

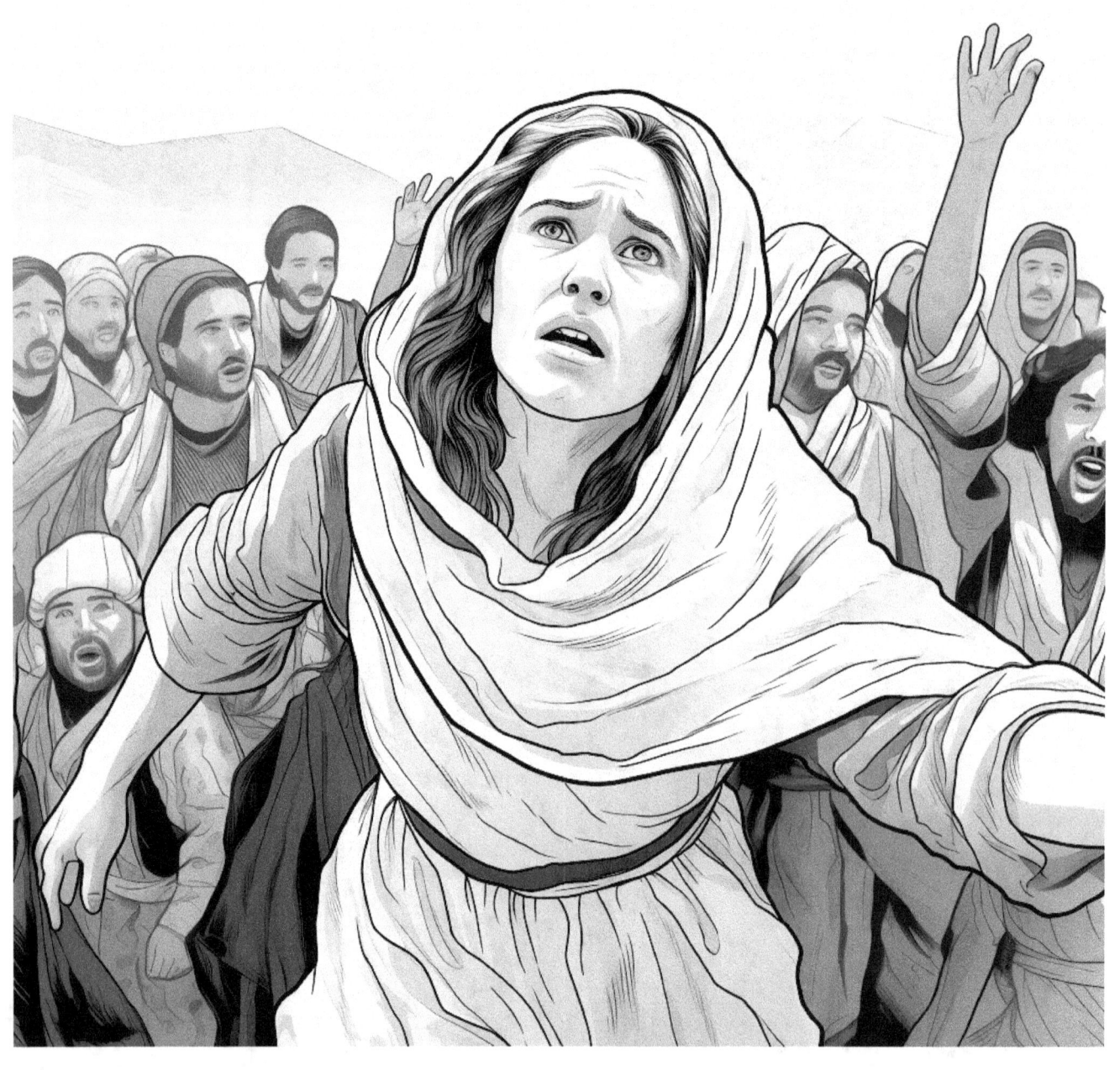

Matthew 9: 21 She said to herself, "If I only touch his cloak, I will be healed."

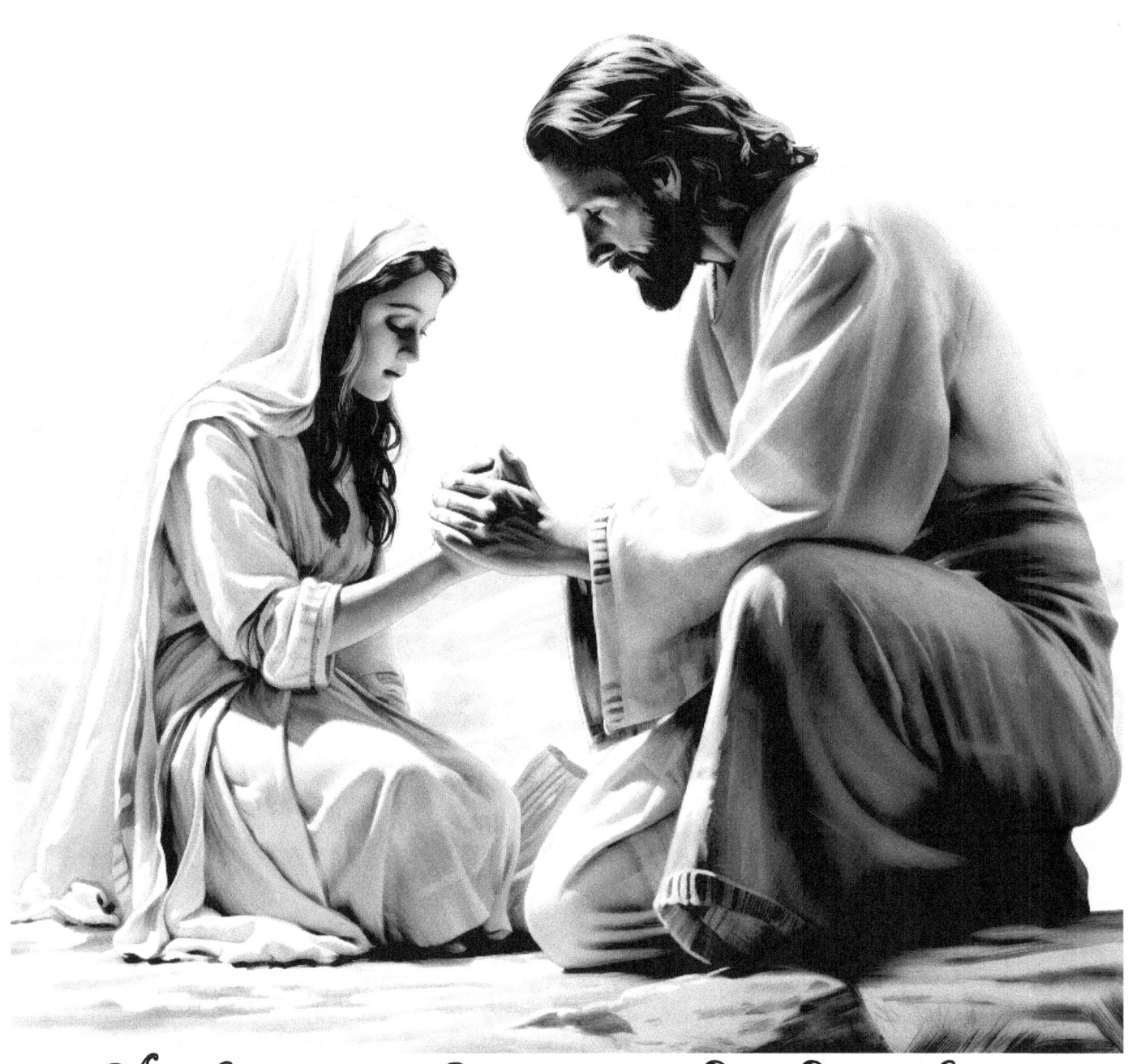

Matthew 9:22 Jesus turned and saw her. "Take heart, daughter," he said, "your faith has healed you." And the woman was healed at that moment.

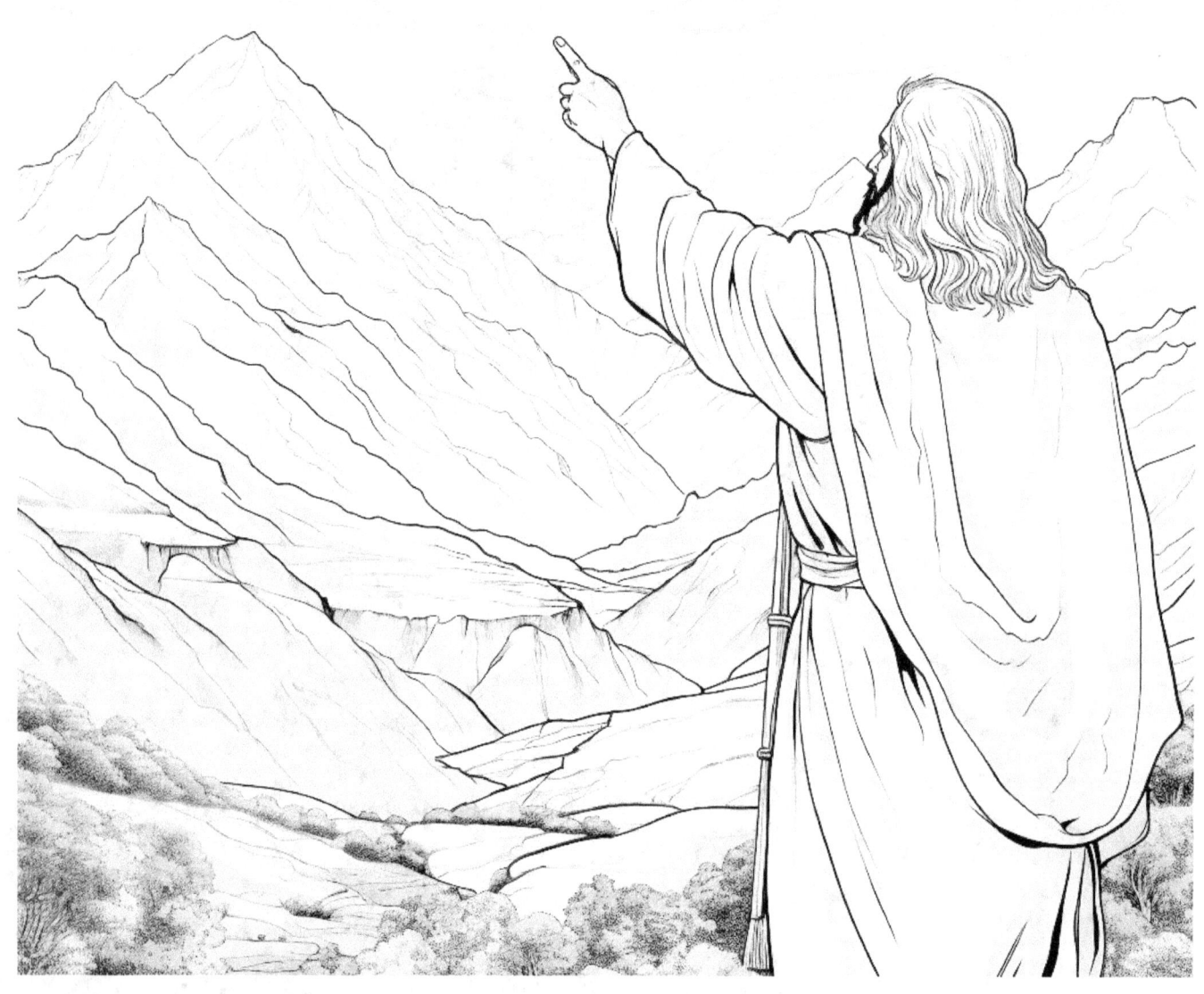

Matthew 17:20 He replied, "Because you have so little faith. Truly I tell you, if you have faith as small as a mustard seed, you can say to this mountain, 'Move from here to there,' and it will move.

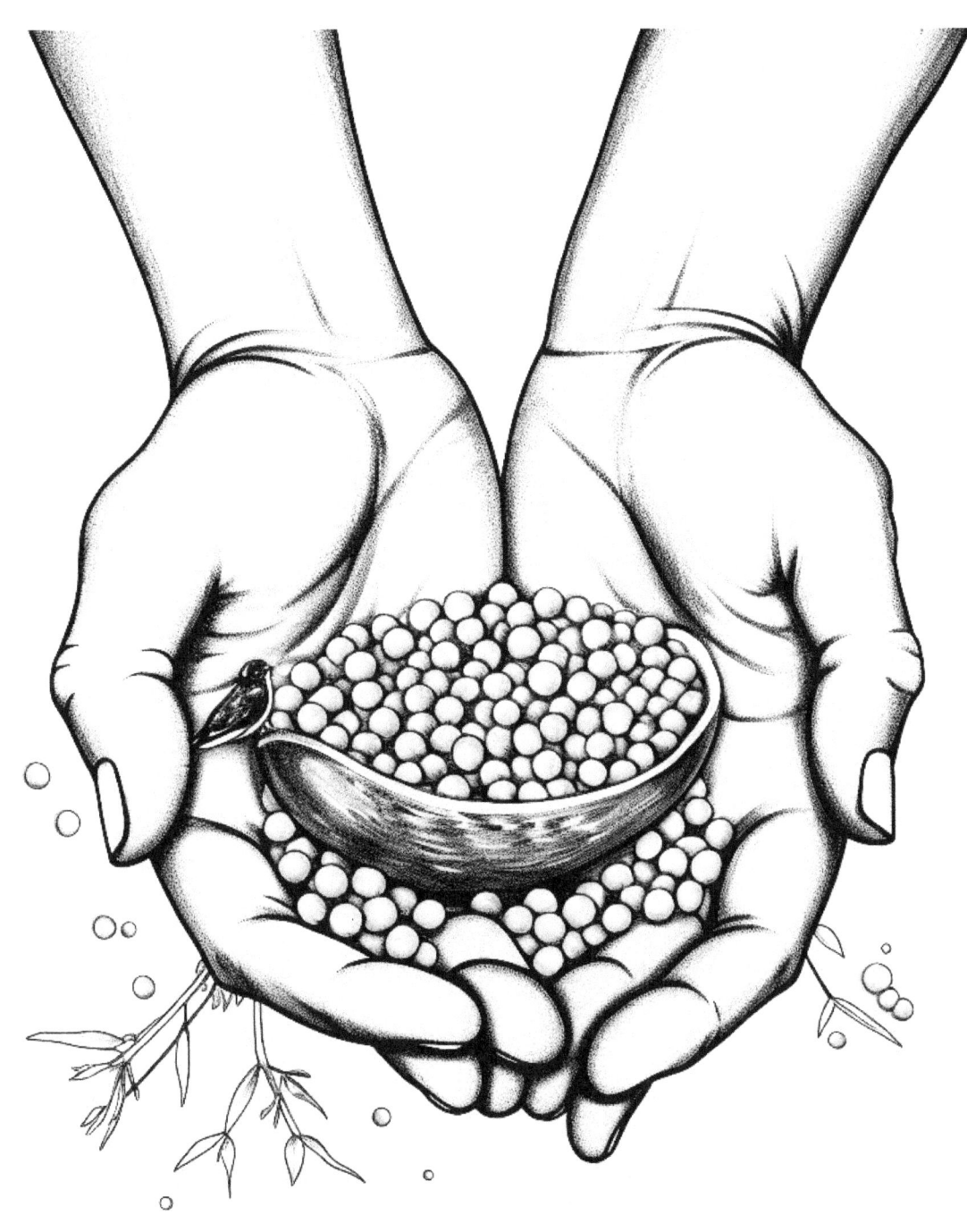

Matthew 17:20 cont... Nothing
will be impossible for you.

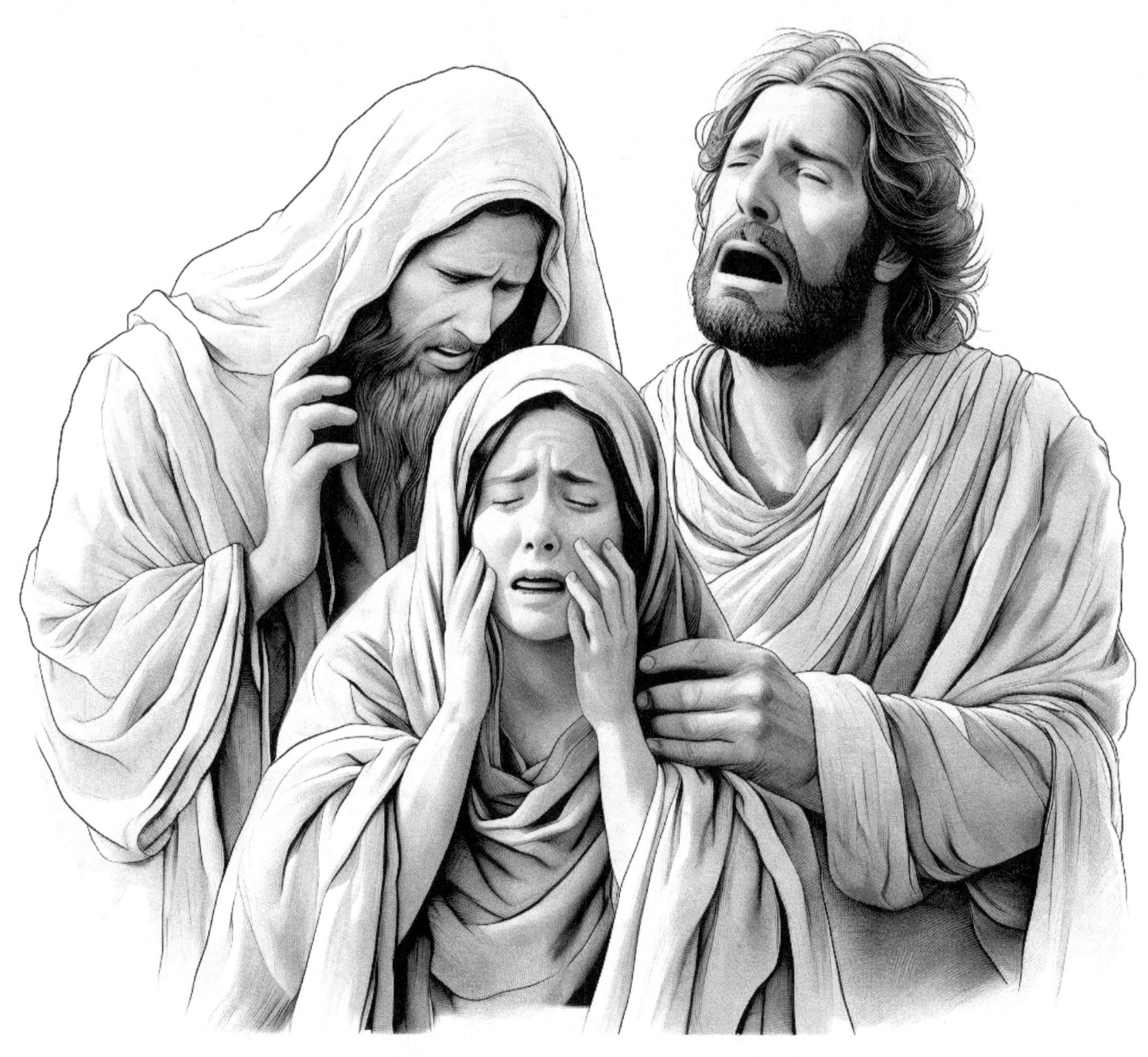

Mark 5:39 He went in and said to them, "Why all this commotion and wailing? The child is not dead but asleep."

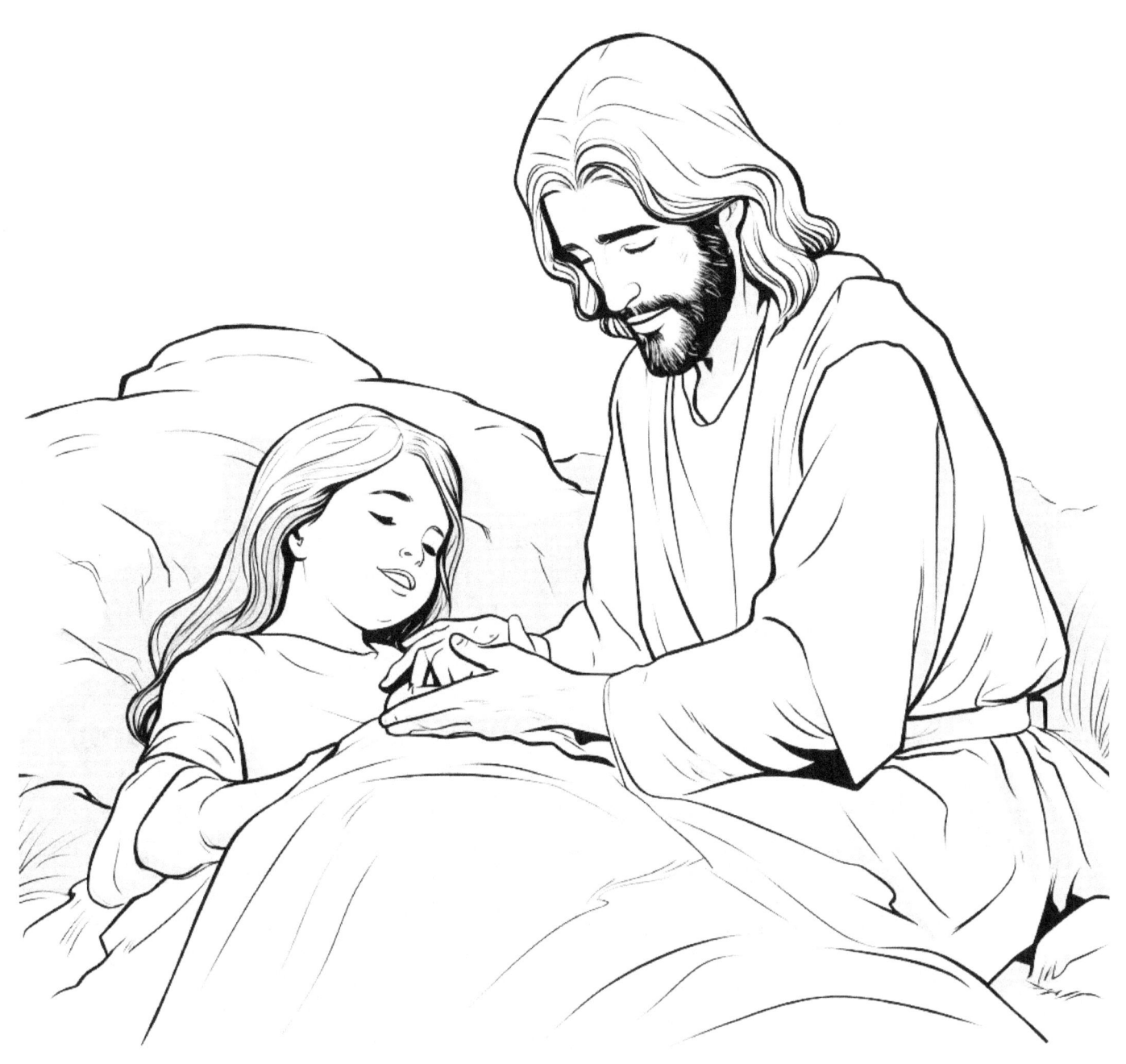

Mark 5:41 He took her by the hand and said to her, "Talitha koum!" (which means "Little girl, I say to you, get up!").

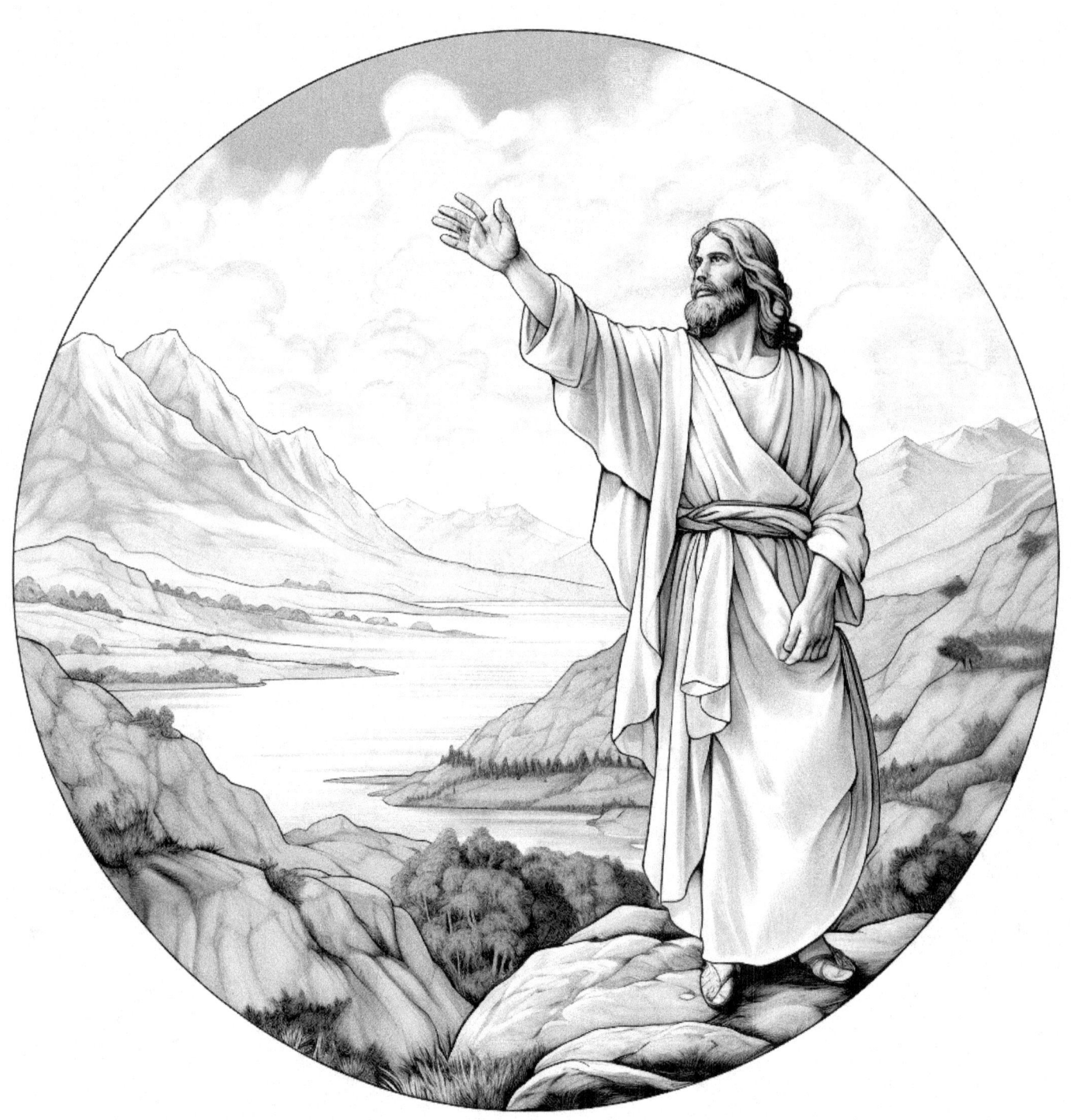

Mark 11:22 "Have faith in God," Jesus answered. "Truly I tell you if anyone says to this mountain "Go throw yourself into the sea and does not doubt in their heart but believes that what they say will happen it will be done for them.

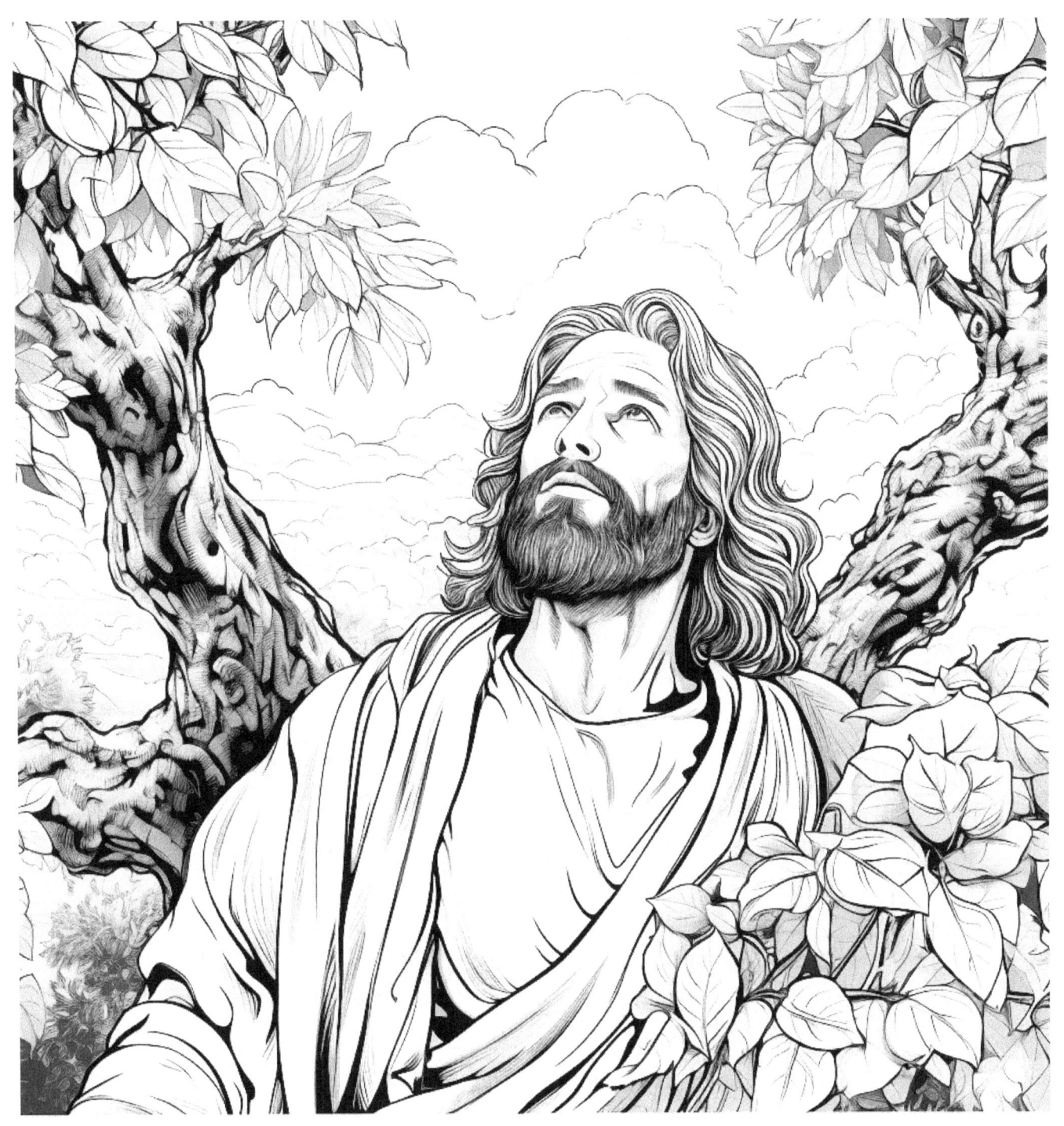

Mark 11:24 Therefore I tell you, whatever you ask for in prayer, believe that you have received it, and it will be yours. 25 And when you stand praying, if you hold anything against anyone, forgive them, so that your Father in heaven may forgive you your sins."

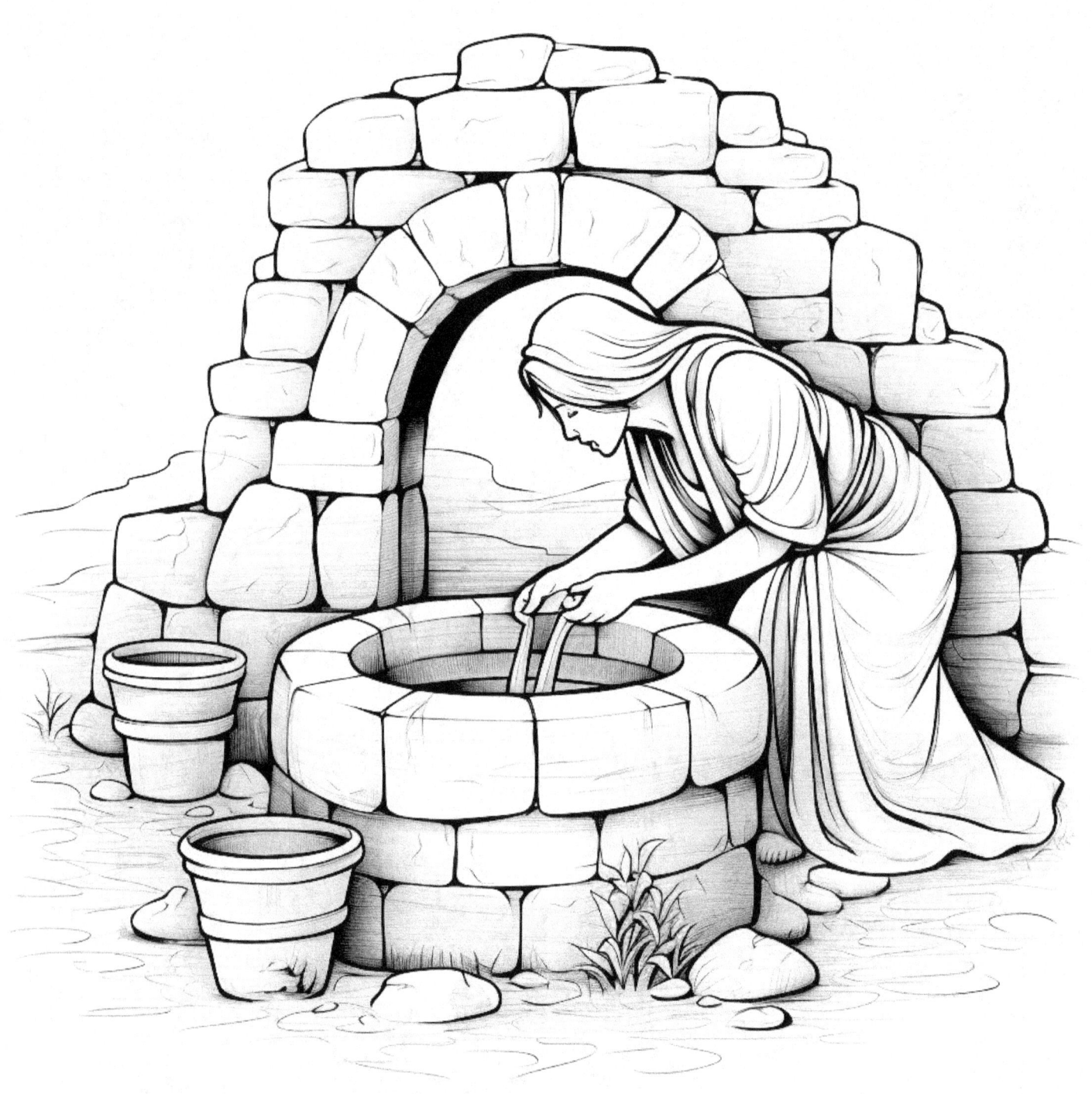

John 4: 13 Jesus answered, "Everyone who drinks this water will be thirsty again,

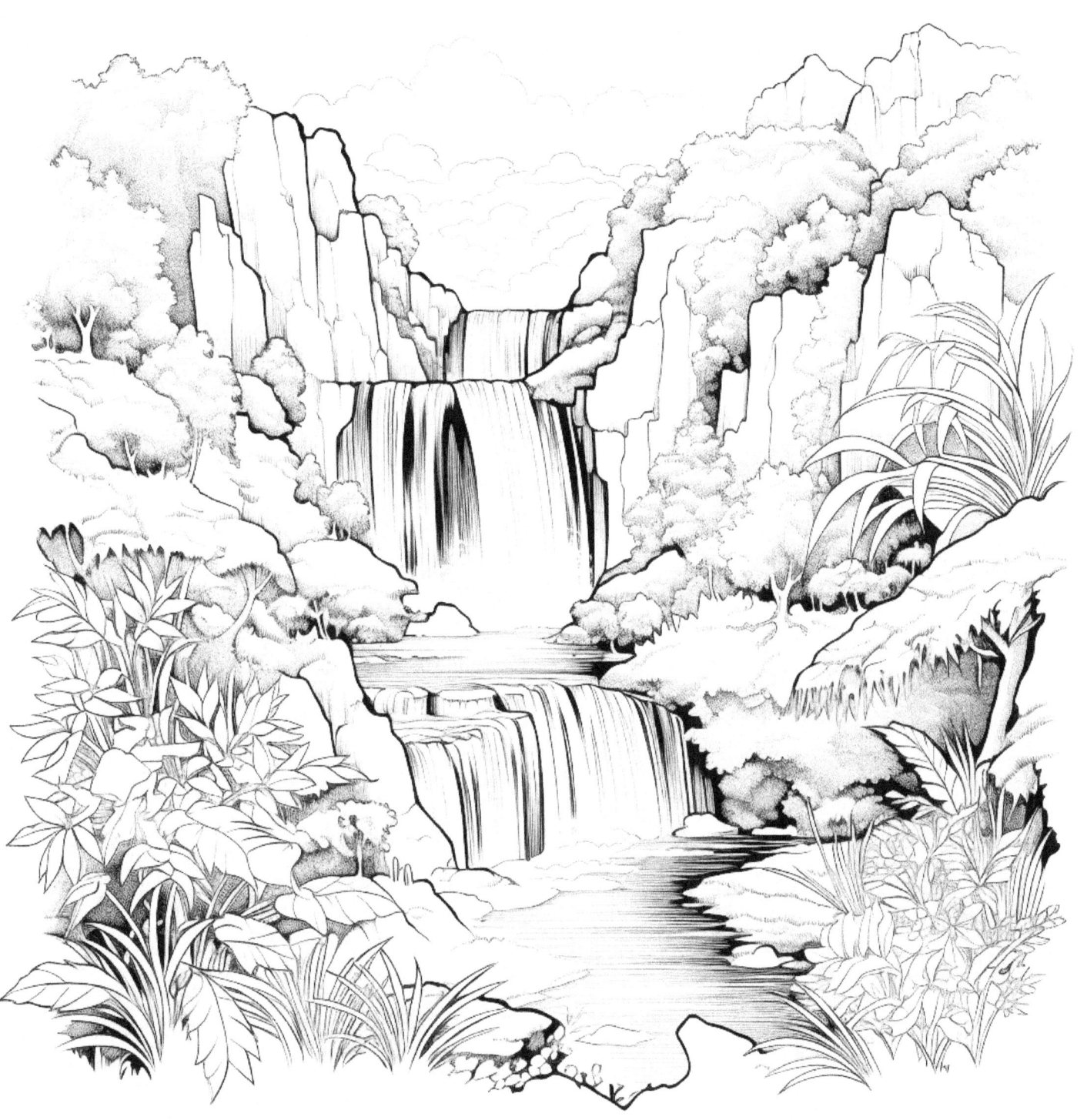

John 4:14 but whoever drinks the water I give them will never thirst. Indeed, the water I give them will become in them a spring of water welling up to eternal life."

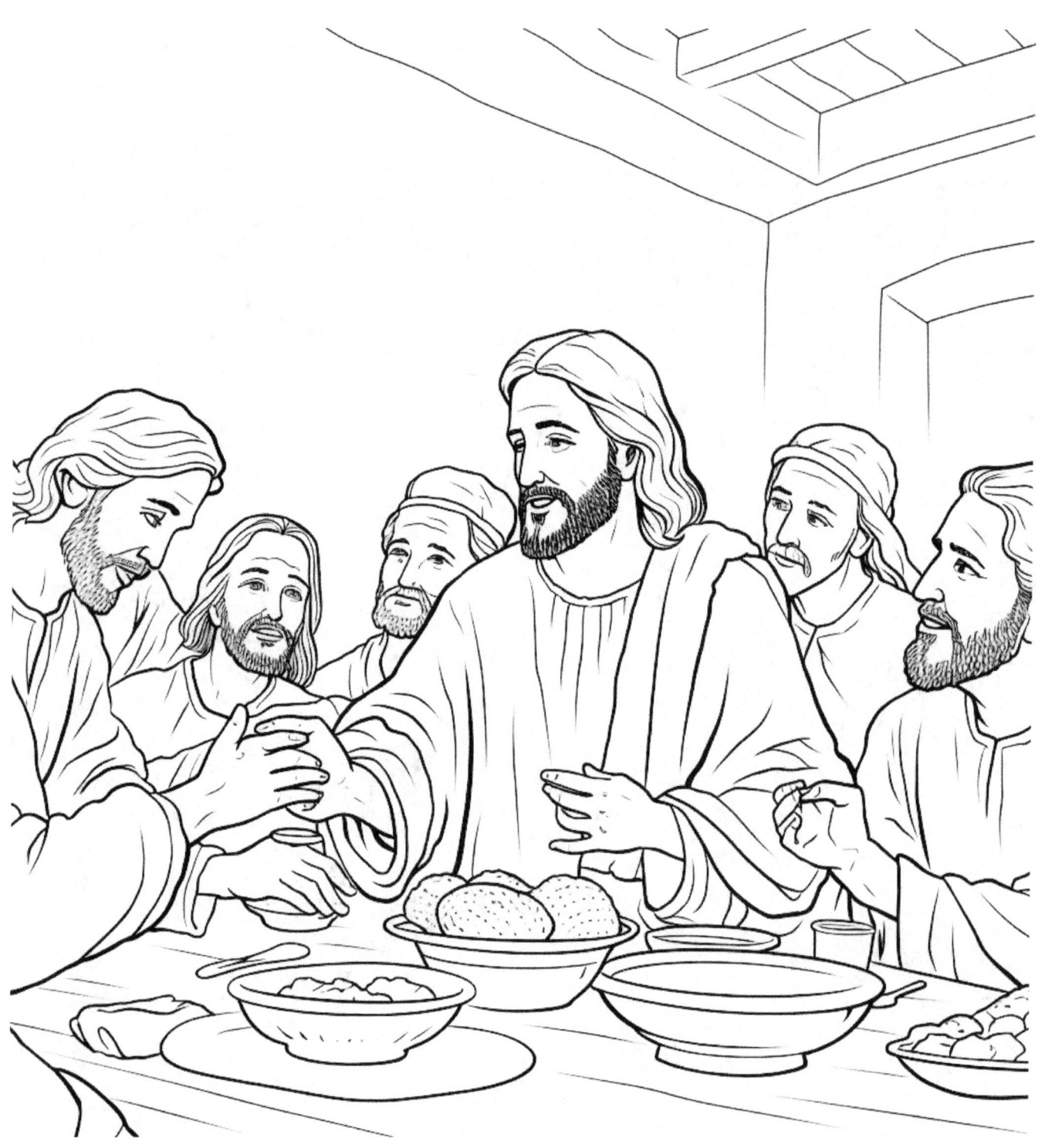

Matthew 26:26 While they were eating, Jesus took bread, and when he had given thanks, he broke it and gave it to his disciples, saying, "Take and eat; this is my body."

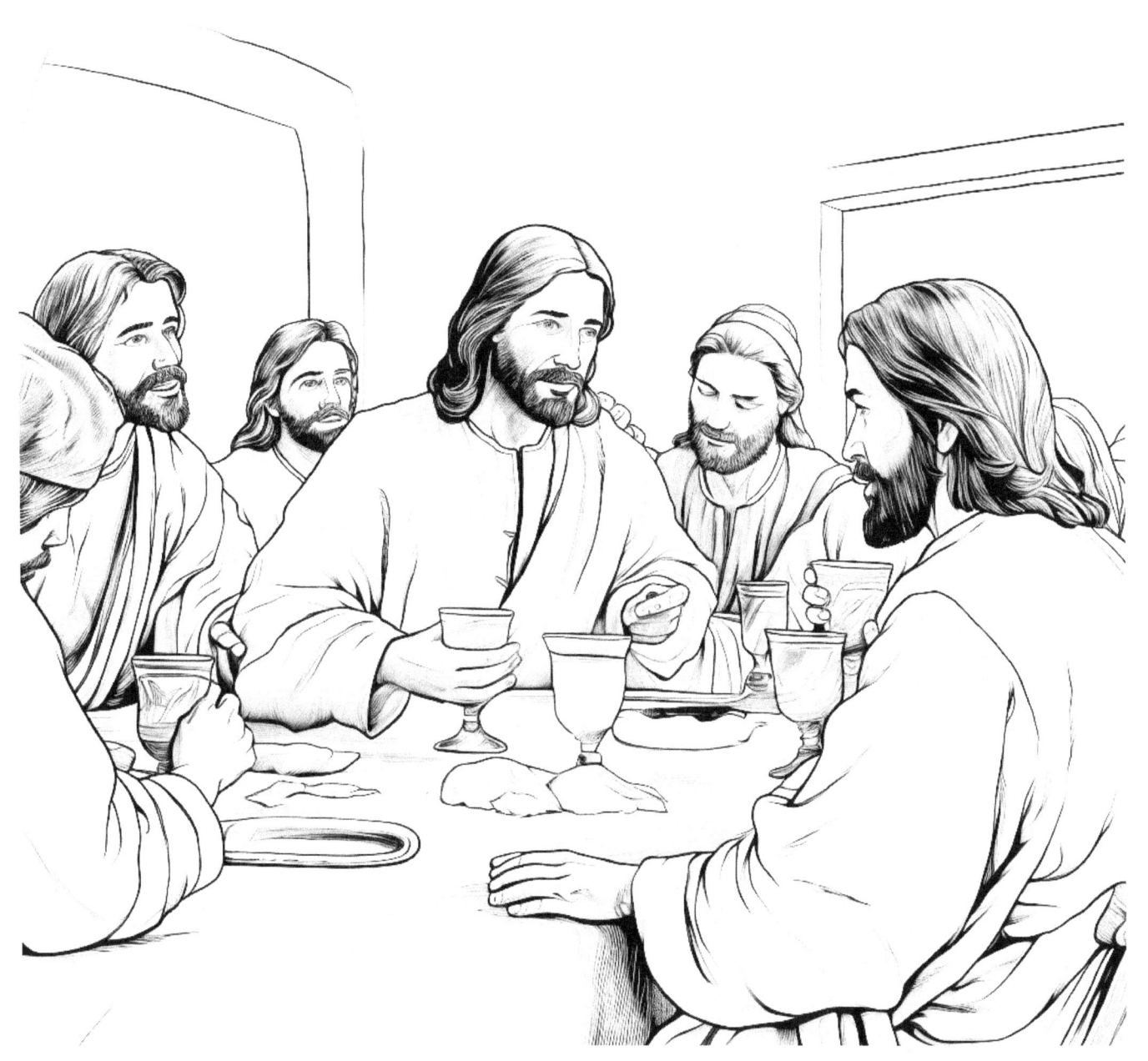

Matthew 26:27 Then he took a cup, and when he had given thanks, he gave it to them, saying, "Drink from it, all of you. 28 This is my blood of the covenant, which is poured out for many for the forgiveness of sins.

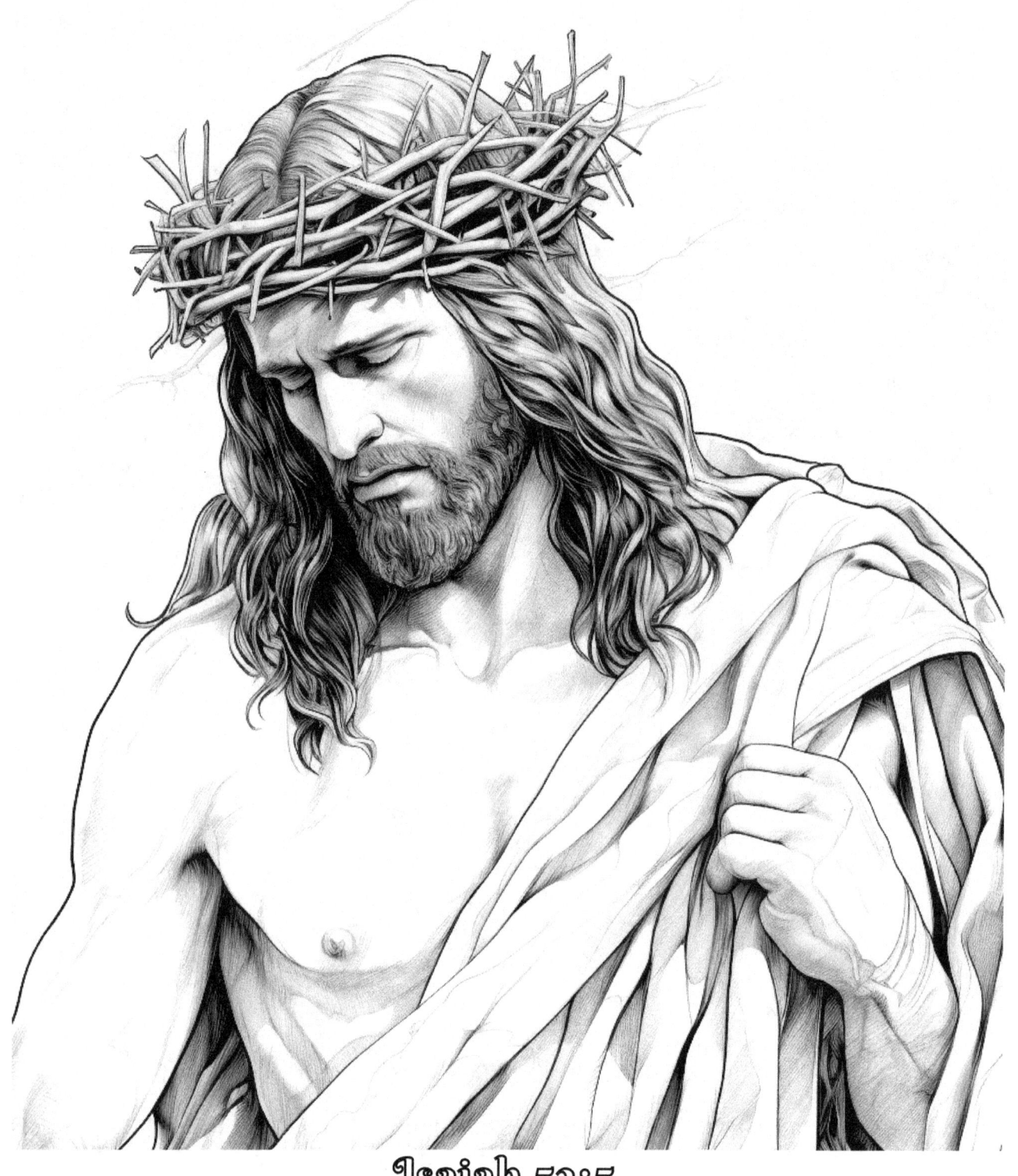

Isaiah 53:5

But he was wounded for our transgressions, he was bruised for our iniquities: the chastisement of our peace was upon him; and with his stripes we are healed.

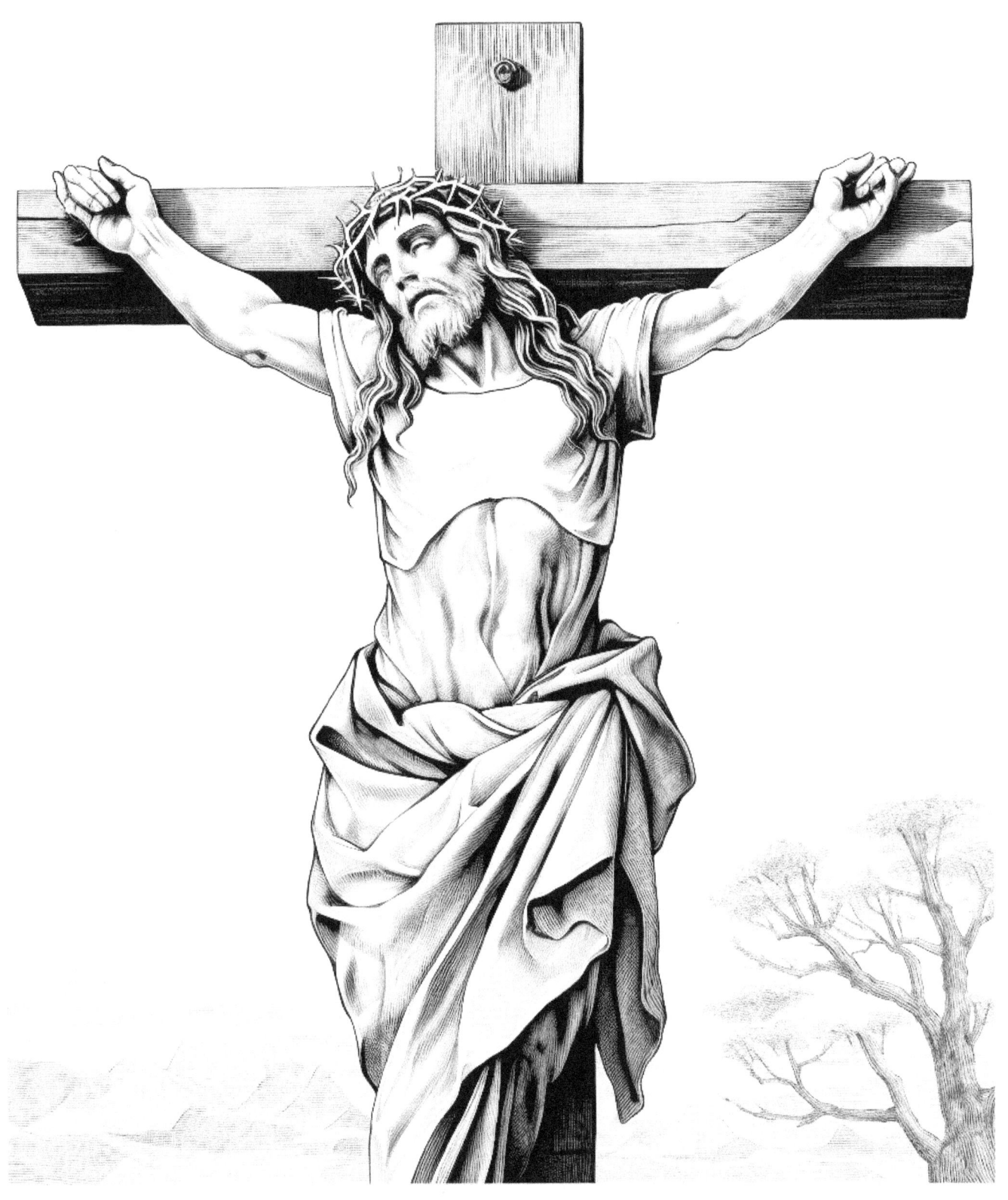

Matthew 27:50 And Jesus cried out again with a loud voice, and yielded up His spirit.

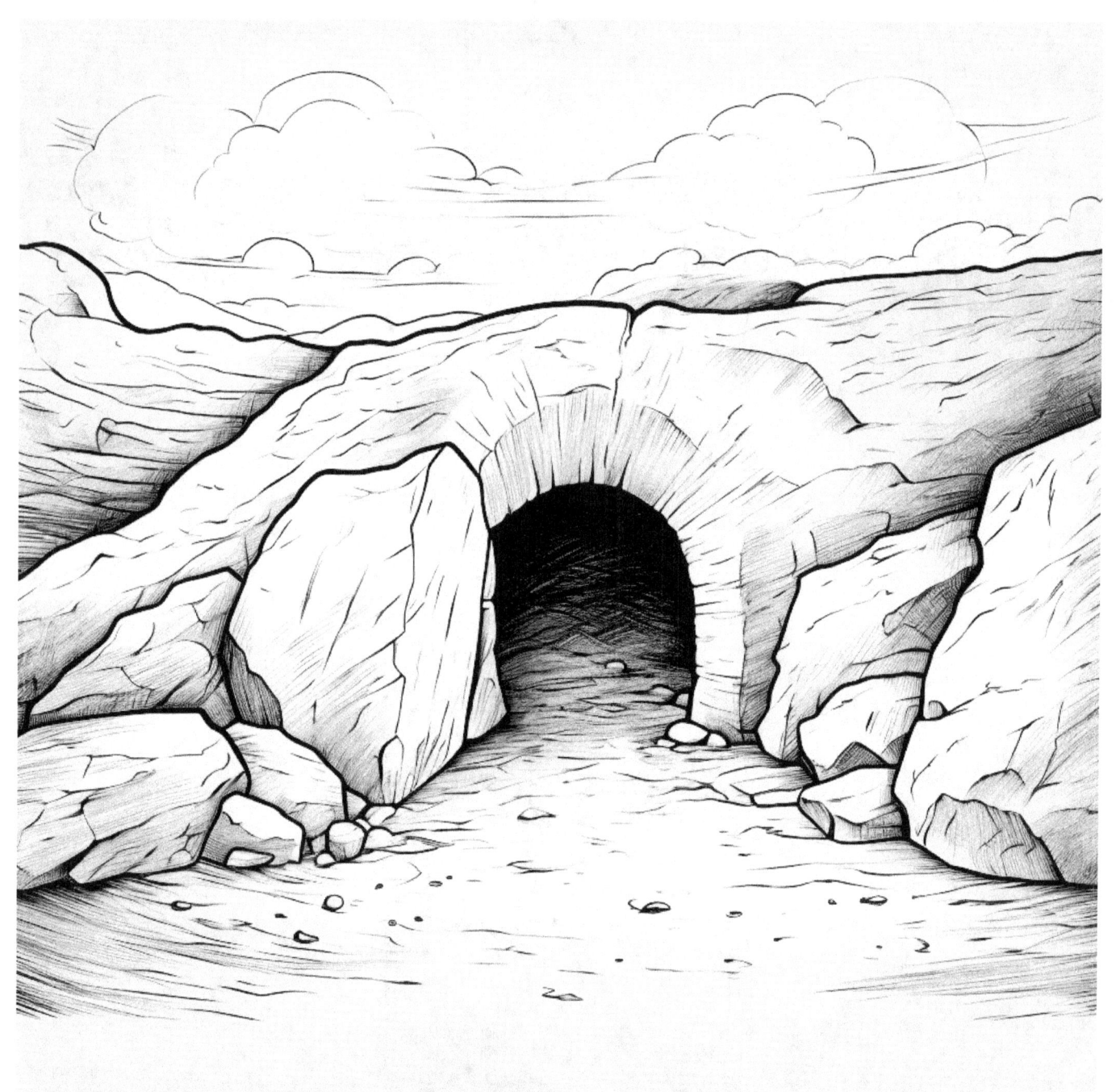

5 And the angel answered and said unto the women, Fear not ye: for I know that ye seek Jesus, which was crucified. 6 He is not here: for he is risen, as he said. Come, see the place where the Lord lay.

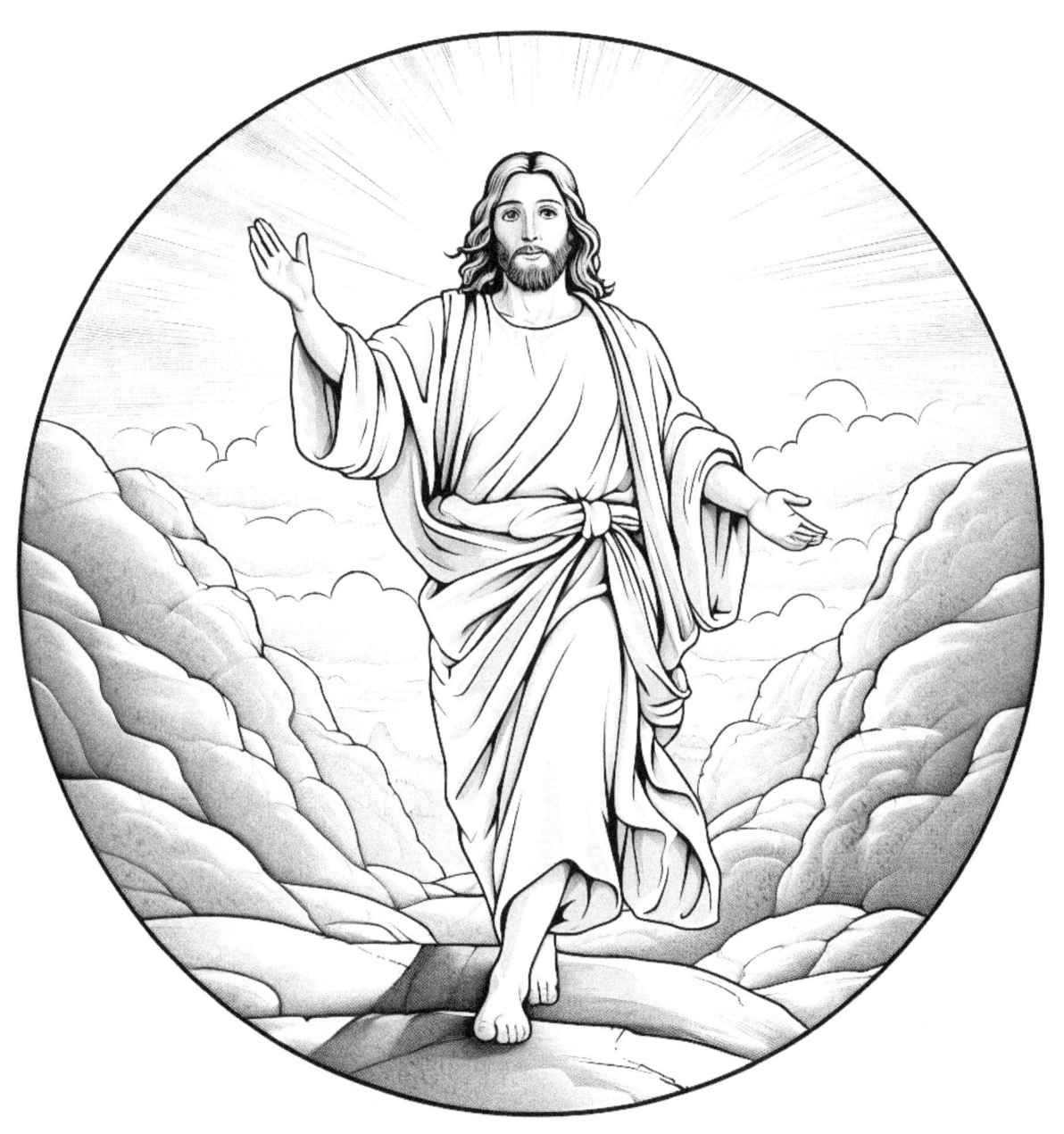

18 And Jesus came and spake unto them, saying, All power is given unto me in heaven and in earth   19 Go ye therefore, and teach all nations, baptizing them in the name of the Father, and of the Son, and of the Holy Ghost:

20 Teaching them to observe all things whatsoever I have commanded you: and, lo, I am with you always, even unto the end of the world.   Amen.